Tales from a Good Life

Ken Dye

The events in this book are from the recollections of the author and are authentically represented from the author's point of view.

First printing November 2013 (200 copies)

Cover design by Victoria Hawley

Cover photo: Ken Dye, Arctic Ocean marine salvage project (September 1970)

We all have the ability to become connected to a positive spiritual presence; we simply need to learn how to listen—and follow the guidance we are given.

Some of Ken's grandkids at the cabin in Halfway, Oregon (2012)

This book is dedicated to my children, grandchildren, and great-grandchildren. May it give them a picture of my life and how I became the person I am. More importantly, may it provide them the motivation to find their own spiritual voice and to follow it.

Table of Contents

PART 5: TIME FOR A CHANGE · 167

PART 7: WHAT DOES IT MEAN? · 221

Photographs

Introduction

This is the story of a man who has been guided throughout his life by a spiritual force. A voice.

I've known Ken Dye for fourteen years. My husband and I live on a boat at one of his moorages. Most mornings and evenings, one or more of the moorage regulars will drift into Ken's floating home apartment at the bottom of the ramp for coffee or a sundowner. Over the years we heard his remarkable stories of salvage diving in the Arctic Ocean and South America, tales of searching for gold, of pulling a sailboat out of the sand and bringing it back to life, tales of miraculous shots that helped feed his family and others, and tales of building businesses, homes, boats and moorages.

What he didn't always tell us was that behind these tales was a spiritual presence that guided him to accomplish what a man could not do on his own.

In 2004 Ken printed some of his stories in a small blue booklet titled "Tales from a Good Life." People who read the stories wanted more and over the next few years various people helped Ken document additional stories. I offered to sort through Ken's stories and attempt to shape them into a coherent, readable tale. In the course of this work Ken retold the original stories and added many new ones. Ken did a remarkable job of telling and retelling the stories the same way—in the retelling he may have added or deleted details, but the story remained the same. This gave me confidence that he was not making anything up—that what he told me was what happened as he experienced it.

It was a toss-up whether to tell the stories in chronological order or to group them by theme. In the end, we chose to group the stories by theme as the main purpose of this book—to describe one man's experience with a spiritual presence—is easier to see when the reader sees, as Ken eventually did after looking at the cumulative effect of his successes, that his many successes are the result of a presence outside of himself.

As much as possible I retained Ken's mannerisms of speech; such as his use of the term "spiritual" as a noun instead of an adjective (spiritual v. spiritual presence.)

Wherever practicable, I validated historical events (see footnotes).

Ken is okay with the stories being entertaining—and they are—but his primary goal is to show how spiritual connections in his life guided him in that life. He wants others to see how the spiritual world exists and guides us through our lives. He is concerned that small blood clots are interfering with his memory and the stories—and the message—will be lost.

This book is not intended to portray Ken's entire life; this selection of stories focuses on the parts of his life that were directly or indirectly influenced by a spiritual presence. Often the presence of a guiding hand was not obvious at the time, but, in retrospect, sometimes years later, it became obvious to him—from the way one experience led to the other—that the cumulative effect of these experiences was not an accident.

Whether you believe Ken is guided by external forces, has a strong innate sense of purpose that drives him, or is just plain lucky, is up to you. In any case, this extended version of Tales from a Good Life offers insights into a remarkable man's experiences with life and a spiritual presence.

Victoria Hawley, aboard *M/V Kaizen*, November 2012—November 2013

Foreword

THE FIRST TIME I heard the voice was in the fourth grade. The words were clear and precise. I knew they were in my head, but, at the time, I thought this was normal—that everyone had messages guiding them.

It was three years after the end of WWII. Our fourth grade teacher introduced a lesson about occupations. I was fascinated with this topic because I had never thought, *Someday I'll be a grownup and have a job. Someday I'll be as big as my dad.* My dad was 5'7" and the tallest man in his family. As I sat in class, I imagined I was going to be a big guy with an exciting job.

I was a very secure little boy. I had two loving parents, a wonderful sister and a fun younger brother. We lived in a great community. I figured life would always be like this.

The teacher told the class, "You are all going to be grownups one day. You will need a job, an occupation. You have to prepare yourselves."

Wow! I'd never thought about it like that—I was having so much fun being a little boy. Now I thought, *One day I'll have a job. I wonder what I'll do?*

Just as I recognized the thought, I heard a voice. A very clear, concise voice. The voice said, "You are going to be a professional diver."

I was nine years old living in Ashland, a small town in southern Oregon, a couple of hundred miles from the ocean. It was 1948. I had no idea what a professional diver was. Nevertheless, the voice told me I was going to be a professional diver and I believed that message. I had no reason not to. I assumed everyone had voices telling them what was going to happen. From that moment on, I repeated to myself what the voice said: I knew I was going to be a professional diver. [1]

The voice has spoken to me a few times since then, always in the same clear, concise way. I also received "knowledge" messages where I knew something to be

---

[1] The Aqua-Lung was invented in Paris during the winter of 1942–1943 by the engineer Émile Gagnan and the *lieutenant de vaisseau* (ship-of-the-line lieutenant) Jacques Cousteau, both of France. 1948 (the same year Ken was told he was going to be a professional diver) Siebe Gorman was making aqualungs of the type nicknamed 'Tadpoles'. http://en.wikipedia.org/wiki/Aqua-lung

true without knowing how I knew. And I have been able to do things that I do not believe to be humanly possible.

These experiences reinforced my belief in the human connection with a spiritual world. I am not talking about religion. I always believed in a god that was over everything, and that the spirit world and its messages came from God, but I believe man has flawed religion. I do not mean that religion is imperfect, but that man has made religion imperfect. Religion in its pure form is a beautiful thing, but when man starts putting his opinion on it, it becomes flawed.

As a teenager I went to several churches to see what they were about. I believe there is no right or wrong way to get there: If you are doing the right thing to help people, and you are doing it the way the spiritual word wants you to, as long as you are not hurting anyone and are doing good along the way, it doesn't matter if you are an atheist or a radical of one sort or another.

After a lifetime of thinking about my experiences, and studying other peoples' experiences with a spiritual presence, I believe that the spirit world is made up of the departed souls of man that have gone through life many times, as we have, and have evolved into a higher entity. I believe there are also negative spirits that get into people's heads. My spiritual messages have always been positive.

I've lived a life like so many other people: Marrying twice, raising children, making money, running a business. Those were all good things. There were difficult times, too. I was a husband and father while still in high school. I taught myself to be a professional diver and played a key role in some of the most difficult salvage operations on the West Coast of North America. I was nearly killed several times, but always escaped, with a broken leg as my one serious injury. I made my deepest dive in a full leg cast while searching for gold. As a hunter, I had special knowledge of where to find game and made miracle shots that I could not consciously replicate. I accomplished most of the goals I set in my youth: I became a professional diver and achieved and maintained financial security. I have close relationships with family and friends that enrich my life.

Through all this was a voice, a spiritual presence, and it guided me.

I recently tried looking back in time to see when the spiritual started "interfering" in my life; when they started to have me do things that it seems I would not normally have done. An early instance comes to mind: When I was a young boy, there was another little boy in our neighborhood that the other kids picked on. Jackie was "different;" he didn't have good parentage and didn't do well in school or with the other kids. I felt bad for him, and after school would go over to his place to play. One day my mom took me aside and said, "Kenny, you know people judge us by the company we keep. You have to be careful about who you choose for your friends."

Mom hadn't said his name, but I knew whom she meant. I answered, "But Mom, if I'm not Jackie's friend, Jackie won't have a friend."

I believe the spiritual was working through me so Jackie would have a friend.

For several months I have been having some pretty serious memory issues (caused, the doctors believe, from a series of small clots) and have difficulty with both short-term and long-term memory. However, the memory of this incident involving Jackie is crystal clear, as are all the memories when I heard or felt a spiritual presence—I can remember every voice message and knowledge message as clearly as the day I received them; there is something special about these memories that makes my mind treat them differently than other memories.

The most precious gift I can offer to others is an opportunity to develop relationships with the spiritual world as I have; that is why I am writing this book. My concern is that young people, at this particular time, lack a spiritual connection. You see them on the street or on TV; our young people are in trouble. They have trouble getting jobs. They are over eating. Young people coming out of high school and college are oblivious to the spiritual world; they come from families with no spiritual foundation. Perhaps this book may help someone get started; to let a young person see that if a regular guy like me can have a spiritual connection, they can, too. They just have to learn to listen and be ready to do what the spiritual guides them to do.

As a family, we did not regularly attend church. When I was a kid, I went to Sunday School now and then to see what it was about and meet people. As kids, we knew enough from our families and going to church to know a spiritual power was there and to believe in something outside of ourselves. If I can present myself as just a regular guy, someone who believes that if you ask for help you will get it. Now, believe me, you don't get it handed to you on a platter, you have got to do the right thing to get what you want. It's about living a good life. It's about doing the right thing for the right reason.

I worry, though, that people will read my stories and think it's my ego talking. All these stories are true and as factual as I can recall them. I keep asking the spiritual, *Should I be writing this book?* The question is always on my mind. I haven't gotten a direct answer. Or maybe I have... about the time Victoria and I started on this version of the book, I was driving down McLoughlin Boulevard heading home. There were two lanes of traffic and I was in the right lane; traffic was heavy. The car in front of me had a license plate with three numbers followed by three letters—the last three letters spelled DYE. *That's kind of cute,* I thought. A car in the left lane pulled alongside the first car—the last three letters on this license plate spelled out the word EGO. It may have just been a coincidence... Perhaps it was a warning. Maybe it was an answer.

As you will see—they can communicate with me in many ways!

Part 1: Early Life

The pale yellow house at 203 N Mountain Avenue, Ashland, Oregon (1957)

Chapter 1: Growing Up

EXCEPT FOR hearing a voice, I was a pretty normal kid for my time and place. I was born near Los Angeles in Wilmington, California, on February 6, 1939. I was named Wayne Kenneth Jr., after my father, and am the middle of three children. Dad was called Wayne so I was called Ken. My sister, Deanne, is two years older and Norman was born a couple of years after I was. I was raised by two wonderful parents. My mother was a very loving, caring lady. I never heard her say an unkind word about anyone. Dad was a fun-loving guy who took us hunting and fishing.

Dad taught us to love life. To enjoy life. Everybody loved him. He was a character. As a family, we always had fun. We fished and took care of the cows and chickens on the Dye Farm. But I was never sure what he thought of me.

All during high school I came home in the evenings after football practice, or whatever I was doing, and milked our two cows; that was my responsibility. Dad milked them in the mornings. There was a milk separator on the back porch; we bottled some of the milk and sold it.

I hated milking the cows; it interfered with my fun and, to my teenaged way of thinking, became a total nuisance. After a while I got to milking them pretty aggressively so I could finish the job fast. Really fast.

One afternoon Dad pulled into the driveway much earlier than usual. He was in kind of a foul mood that day. He sat down at the kitchen table and lit a cigarette. Every single night I can remember, Dad came into the house, poured a cup of coffee, sat down at the kitchen table, and lit a cigarette. Nobody bothered him; it was his time to take the work at the propane company off of his shoulders and ease into the evening.

Dad was sitting at the kitchen table when I went out to milk the cows. There was something important going on at school and I remember thinking, *I gotta get this done.* I milked those two cows extra fast and both pails were full. They were overflowing. When I came back to the house with the pails, Dad was still sitting there; he hadn't finished his cigarette yet.

"You need to strip them cows," he said. A cow will produce as much milk as you ask her to and, if you back off, she'll start producing less until she dries up altogether.

"Dad, I did."

"Ken, you couldn't have. You haven't been out long enough. I haven't finished my cigarette. You couldn't have stripped them."

I said again, "I did."

We had a third bucket; Dad grabbed it up.

"Come on," he said.

He was going to show me that I hadn't done it properly.

Ken milking the family cow (1942)

As a little kid, I watched Dad milk the cow on the Dye family farm in California.

One day when I was three, after Dad finished milking and left for work, I decided to try it myself: I led the cow back to the stall, put her head in the stanchion, gave her some feed, and sat down with my stool and bucket.

I told Mom about it—she told me not to tell Dad, but to do the same thing that night when he got home; Mom snuck around the barn with our old box camera and took this picture.

We got the cows back into the milking shed, their heads in the feeder with the hay, and Dad sat down on the milking stool, but he couldn't get a drop. Not one drop.

I didn't dare laugh, but I wanted to. I can still see him there pulling on that cow; he thought he had me. I went back into the house. Dad and I were close, but very different in temperament.

When I was born, my father, Wayne Kenneth Dye, Sr. was the skipper of a wealthy man's yacht. Before I was born and while he was in high school in

Newport Harbor, California, Dad joined the Sea Scouts and learned to navigate and work on boats. The Sea Scouts were a good group.[2] Just after Dad graduated from high school in the 1930's, a boat owner came to Newport looking to hire Sea Scouts to crew on his yacht. Wayne and his buddies signed on to the *Stranger*, a 230-foot motor vessel outfitted with gigantic holding tanks filled with sea water; the owner's mission was to go to the South Pacific to catch tropical fish and bring them back to the States to sell.[3]

This was before WWII. Unbeknown to the owner and crew, the U.S. Government knew trouble was coming. In preparation for the war, the entire crew was taken on as spies for the government. I don't know what kind of information they were looking for as they gathered tropical fish, but it was an exciting time for all of them and the young sailors had fabulous times. Hearing about Dad's adventures was a major part of our lives. We have albums full of pictures the Sea Scouts took of women in grass skirts with no tops

Winnie and Wayne Dye (1937)

Mom and Dad met at a party before Dad left for the South Pacific. He wrote to her and another woman while he was gone. When Dad returned home, he picked Mom. Mom and Dad were married April 5, 1937, in Long Beach, California. (Many, many years later, we kids wanted to give them a 50th anniversary party. Deanne looked up the date in Grandma's bible to be sure we had it right. It seems she was born the same year our parents were married. It had never come up before—we'd always assumed they'd been married longer, and Deanne decided to ask Mom about it. She sat Deanne down and said, "Deanne, I got

---

[2] (Wayne must have been in the Sea Scouts around 1934.) 1932 Five Ships, 75 Sea Scouts in Orange County Council. 1935 First annual Region XII Sea Scout Rendezvous held in Newport Beach, Nov. 29- Dec. 1. 1937 The Orange County Council signed a 25-year lease with the City of Newport Beach for 100' of bay front.
http://www.newportseabase.org/history/

[3] Frederick E. Lewis brought (the Stranger) his 230-foot, 297-ton diesel yacht from New York to Long Beach, California in 1935-36, with an extended visit to Galápagos along the way. A group of Orange County California Sea Scouts served in the crew, and in Galápagos collected iguanas, penguins and other birds which were subsequently given to the San Diego Zoo.
http://www.flickr.com/photos/k38shawn/sets/72157625443383500/

something to tell you. Grandma's dates are right." Until then, no one paid any attention to the year they were married. Deanne was glad to find out about her "premature" status at fifty rather than when she was in high school.)

When he came back to Newport Harbor after the South Pacific trip, Dad went on a smaller yacht as skipper for a big corporate attorney in Los Angeles. He did all the maintenance on board, and, when the owners were ready to board, Dad's job was to take them where they wanted to go. When the owners and their guests were done playing, Dad took them safely back to port.

When the war broke out, the government confiscated the yacht for shore patrol and Dad lost his job. He was around 25 years old with three children and a wife, but no job. Dad soon found work in a shipyard building military ships. At the time, he wasn't eligible for the draft because he was working in support of the war and had three children. He worked at the ship yard for four years. The Germans surrendered May 7, 1945. My parents expected the war to end soon, so Dad quit his job and moved us to Oregon where my mom's parents lived.

Soon after they moved to Oregon, Dad got his draft notice—the war with Germany had ended, but the war with Japan had not. (Ironically, the war with Japan ended four months after the war with Germany, but no one could know that then.) The U.S. military was running out of men, and Dad—now 29-years-old and a father with three kids—had to go back to San Diego for basic training in the Navy.

When he finished basic training, Dad's Commanding Officer announced, "Dye, you have three kids and we're not going to send you out. You are going to stay on the base and we are going to give you a job."

"Well, what's my job?" Dad asked.

"You are going around the base and pick up cigarette butts and sweep the concrete."

It wasn't glamorous and it was a waste of Dad's skills, but he didn't have to go overseas.

In the meantime, Mom had moved us back to Newport Beach to be near Dad. We fixed up a chicken coop at a friend's house and lived in that for a few months until Dad was discharged and we moved back to Ashland. I was around six years old.

For the next twelve years Dad worked for a propane gas company driving trucks and doing installations. The day I graduated from high school, he and Mom took off for southern California, leaving me on the doorstep with a teenaged wife and a baby in my arms. Dad had accepted an offer from an old client—the attorney in L.A. that he had skippered for before the war—to skipper a new boat the attorney was having built in Florida. Dad spent the first few months in Florida overseeing construction of the new yacht. My younger brother, Norman, went with Mom and Dad to California and finished high school at the same school our dad attended. My sister, Deanne, was already married to her husband, Bill, and living in southern California.

When the yacht owner died, Dad went on to skipper a boat for Barney Morris, who at the time was the ninth-richest man in the United States. Barney had a resort at Lake Sherwood in southern California. After a few years of skippering for Barney, Dad wanted to do something else and asked for a job at Barney's resort as manager.

When Norman graduated high school, he started working at the resort, too.

A few years later, I purchased the Sportcraft Landing boat moorage at Oregon City below Willamette Falls on the Willamette River. I needed managers, so I offered my parents ownership in the moorage if they would move to Oregon and be the managers. They accepted my offer and Norman stayed on as manager at the resort at Lake Sherwood.

Mom and Dad moved into the manager's house at Sportcraft. While I went on salvage job dives, they ran the moorage. I used the money I made diving to expand the moorage. I'll tell you more about this later.

After work, the folks would have a drink in the evening. The rule was you couldn't drink on the job, but, after a few years, Dad got into the habit of quitting early and started tapping it while Mom kept working. Then it got to be more and more and he got loud and obnoxious on the docks.

Finally, I had to have a talk with him. It was agonizing.

"If you continue to be a problem on the docks," I told him, "I will physically remove you. You have to get your drinking under control."

Mom was there, too, and I could see she was crying. I didn't know what to do. I didn't realize I was hurting my mother—that she saw it as me kicking them out of their home. They knew when I decided something—that was it; I meant it.

Sometimes you have to do things that are hard.

Mom and Dad discussed it; he never quit drinking entirely, but he cut way back and after that we had some really good times together.

My mom, Winifred (Winnie) Dye, was a very loving mother. While Dad worked, Mom took care of us. My entire life I've never heard anyone say a negative word about my mother—never! It's true. She was surrounded by friends and family all of her life.

My mom had great insight. She was intuitive—I guess you would say spiritually connected. She never spoke of it, but over the years it was plain to see there was something special about her. She was not a particularly outgoing person, but people wanted to be around her. People were attracted to her.

Dolly Flagg Baker (1941)

When she was young, Mom's parents divorced. Grandma Baker never remarried. She was a very spiritual being—a practical nurse who radiated kindness. Whenever she came for a visit and Sunday rolled around, she would find a local church to go to. After the divorce, Grandma couldn't take care of Mom, so Mom went to live with Grandpa Baker, who had a good job.

Grandpa Baker remarried and as kids we had two Grandma Bakers—Grandma Dolly and Grandma Dorothy. Grandma Dolly, Mom's mother, was a reserved woman. Grandma Dorothy was more fun loving, which is probably what attracted Grandpa to her. Grandpa and Grandma Dolly remained friends and would visit when they were in town at the same time.

My parents' first house in Ashland was near town. For my last three years of high school, we moved to a second home that was a nice, older two-story house on a couple of acres on the edge of town (see picture beginning of this section). The exterior of the house was off white, almost a pale yellow. You could say the house was pretty conventional in all respects: single bath, three bedrooms upstairs, and one down. The front porch of the house had railings, but the back porch was enclosed. That's where we kept the milk jugs, pails, and separator.

We had a chicken coop, the two milk cows, and a large garden. When we sat down to dinner, we took great pride that we bought so little at the grocery store. The neighborhood houses were spread out on lots of about an acre each. Everybody sat around their kitchen tables for dinner. The previous owner of our house had built a kitchen extension. The old kitchen was where we had the table and chairs. A big wood stove in the dining area was our main heating. Instead of a fireplace, we had a modern, chrome, combination wood-burning and propane-burning kitchen stove where we could cook on either side using wood or gas.

We got a lot of wood from the mills left over after the boards were trimmed. They were large, fifteen-inch pieces perfect for the stove. We called these stoves trash burners. They put out a lot of heat.

(Mills had trash burners, too, but mill burners were two or three stories high and shaped like wigwams. On my way to the cabin I built in Halfway, Oregon, I pass by an old wigwam burner. When I have a young person in the truck with me, I will point to it ask them, "What is that thing?" No one under thirty has got it yet.)

Our neighbors in Ashland grew more hay than they needed and we bought what we needed for the cows from them. One of the neighbors we regularly bought hay from lived across the street. His daughter, Gee Hodgens, was in my class at school. Gee and I met in the first grade. She had an older brother, Bucky, the same age as my sister, Deanne. Gee's little brother, Bobby, was the same age as my brother Norman.

Gee's father, Charlie Hodgens, was my idol. He managed a lumber company in Ashland and had a small farm. He was very kind and everyone respected him. I thought it would be great if I could grow up to be like him.

Gee was 5'4", lightly built, and sweet, like her dad, Charlie, and her mom, Jesse. They were very kind and loving people.

When I was in my thirties and living in Gladstone, Oregon, I went to visit Gee and her folks. Gee was divorced with two kids. After the visit, her father followed me out to my truck. Charlie told me he was concerned about Gee and the kids living alone and asked me to keep an eye on her.

It is very special for a man to ask another man to watch out for his daughter.

Gee and I are still close friends. It's not many people who stay friends for 70 years. I've been lucky to stay friends with several kids from school.

One of these kids was named Richard Whited. I always wanted a BB gun, but at nine Dad said I was too young to have one. One Christmas went by and I saw this kid up the street had a BB gun. Richard was two years older than me and I didn't know him, but if I couldn't have a BB gun, I could make friends with someone who did have one! We were allowed to shoot red headed woodpeckers because they made holes in houses, and sparrows, but we couldn't shoot song birds.

When Richard was in the eighth or ninth grade, he started going out for sports and he was good at it. He was a handsome guy and very popular. Then he came down with an illness—I never knew what it was, but he had a high fever and was home for a long time. I would go see him. When he came out of his illness, Richard had changed—he was fidgety and couldn't sit still; he would walk the streets of Ashland. Just walk, walk, walk. He couldn't sit still in a classroom; he had to walk. No one was mean to him, but, because he was different, his old friends no longer paid attention to him. About this time his parents bought a place out in the country. It was great for Richard because he could hunt squirrels. I'd ride my bike out there and sometimes spend the night. None of my other friends would include him, so I had to set time aside for Richard. We did that for many years. He couldn't study and didn't graduate from High School.

Richard tried to go into the service, but he was too fidgety. After I graduated, I pursued my career and lost track of him. Richard had an older brother who was a professor, but he didn't have much contact with Richard, either. Years later, when I wanted to get in touch with Richard, I couldn't do it—no one knew where he was. One day, out of the blue, Richard called me when I was building Scappoose Moorage, the second of my three moorages. He was in poor health and living in an apartment on disability. Richard had a hard time managing his money, so I helped take care of him. We had some good years after that. I'd take him to Halfway all the time to go hunting. He loved to go coyote hunting.

Chapter 2: First Jobs

As KIDS we didn't have money. When I was about twelve years old, I really wanted a bicycle, but my parents couldn't buy me one. My mom said, "You are going to have to earn the money for the bicycle you want. Your dad and I can't afford to buy one for you."

My mom was pretty smart. She said to me, "Kenny, do you know how to mow lawns?"

"Yeah, I can do that."

We went down to Sam's Mower and Bike Shop. The rotary motor lawnmower had just come out. Mom put $25 down on a new mower. It was a lot of money. The mower cost $75, so she told me, "Okay, you have to go out and get jobs to pay off the $50 we still owe on the mower. For the $25 down payment, you have to take care of our lawn all summer. Then the mower is yours and you can earn money with it."

I was in tall cotton. I soon had customers lined up all over and I worked my butt off. I recall I only got twenty-five or fifty cents or so per lawn. Out of that I still had to pay off the mower and I really wanted a bicycle.

One day I went to Sam's mower and bike shop and told Sam my dilemma. Sam said, "Well, maybe we can figure something out."

He took me behind his shop where I saw a huge pile of bicycle parts: frames, tires, wheels, and handlebars. My eyes were as big as saucers.

"Why don't we build a bicycle for you out of this pile of stuff?"

"Okay."

"Here's the deal. You save up a couple of dollars from your lawn work and you bring it up here to me. I'll put it on your account and then we'll go out to look for a part for your bicycle."

That sounded good to me. Each week I got a wheel or sprocket or frame. After paying off the lawnmower, all the remaining money went into my bicycle. By the end of summer, I had the parts I needed for a very nice bicycle. Sam and I put it together.

It was the kind of experience I would repeat years later when I needed to build equipment for my businesses with no money.

That same summer I wanted a .22 rifle, but my parents couldn't buy one. I went to the local sporting goods store. The owners' son was the same age as I was and we went to school together. They had a rack of old guns for sale. One was an old pump action .22. They wanted $20 and I used my lawn mowing money to buy it.

The next summer I was thirteen and had a fishing pole, the old .22 rifle I'd bought, the bicycle I'd built, and the lawn mower for making money. I wanted to find new places to hunt and fish further from home so I needed to extend my cycling range. One of my buddies said his dad had a motor from an old Whizzer motor bike hanging in the garage.[4] I asked my friend's dad how much he wanted for it.

"Only twenty-five bucks," he said.

'Only!' I worked, scrounged and saved up. When I had the money, I bought the motor and put it on my bicycle. Instantly, it was a motorbike. *Voila!* I had range. Life was good. However, as I soon learned, with more freedom comes more responsibility and danger.

One day I was squirrel hunting with friends. We called ground squirrels 'grey diggers;' they were fun to shoot. We were hunting in a draw full of oak leaves. I wounded a squirrel and he was thrashing through the leaves. He was wounded pretty bad; instead of wasting a shot, I figured I'd catch him with my hands. He was running and suddenly froze so I reached down to pick him up. He wasn't worn out; the squirrel had seen what I hadn't: a large rattler poised to strike. I jumped back and shot the snake instead. It had ten buttons. As a kid, it was the only rattlesnake I ever encountered hunting. I ran into a couple while hunting in Halfway, but never had another close encounter with a rattlesnake.

---

[4] August 1939: Breene-Taylor Engineering, a Los Angeles-based manufacturer of airplane parts, announced the availability of the Whizzer Model "D" Bicycle Motor. This kit sold for $54.95 and included an air-cooled, four-cycle engine that was capable of producing 1.375 horsepower as well as a 2/3 gallon fuel tank. Approximately 1000 Model "D" motors were made and sold. September 1949: In order to keep pace with its new competition, Whizzer released the Model "300" Motor. This new engine had 7/8 in. valves, a more efficient combustion chamber, better cooling, and a higher compression ratio. These changes resulted in a 3 hp engine that could reach speeds of 40 mph. Whizzer sold about 15,000 Model "300" motors at $109.97 each. (Ken doesn't know which model he had, but, since he estimates his bike went about 30 mph, it was probably the Model D.) http://www.whizzermotorbike.com/History.html

At fourteen I started working on the Owens ranch in Valley View a few miles out of town. We ate and slept at the ranch. I worked my ass off bucking hay bales, but I wasn't fully developed physically and didn't do very well. The other kids my age were put to work driving the mowers, which anyone could do.

I guess I was a little old for my age. A pretty girl of sixteen or so helped Viola Owens do the cooking. A bunch of us were outdoors after dark one night playing a game and I caught the girl under a willow tree and kissed her... She said she wished I was a little older.

The next year I went to Southern California and lived with my aunt and uncle and worked several jobs at hamburger stands and such.

Early the following spring, when I was sixteen, I went back to old Henry at the Owen's ranch. He was working on one of the fences. I told him I wanted a job on the hay crew.

"Well, you know, Ken, the last time you weren't very good," he said.

"Yeah, I was too young."

"How old are you now?"

"Sixteen."

"What?!" He said if he'd known I was only fourteen he wouldn't have hired me the first time. This time, he hired me with two other classmates; one had worked on the ranch as a mower when we were fourteen. The three of us hayed the entire ranch, a job which normally took a four or five-person crew. At the end of the season Henry said our crew was the best he'd ever had—I figure I made up for any deficiencies from when I was fourteen.

That summer we went on a cattle drive. I drove a truck with some equipment they needed and we mended fences along the way. The drive was around thirty miles long—from Valley View up the creek. I met up with the drive on Dead Indian Road, where I traded the truck for one of the horses and got to play cowboy for part of the drive.

Toward the end of summer the owners, Henry and Viola, took a vacation. They hired me to do the milking. The ranch had mechanical milkers, so I didn't stress out the cows milking them too fast by hand!

It was a good life with wonderful people like Sam and my parents. I had the bicycle, a rifle, the mower and a business. Much of my life has been similarly blessed with family, friends, tools I made or earned, and my own businesses. It wasn't all easy, but the jobs I had as a kid helped make me who I am today. It's too bad kids today aren't allowed to work hard. Working gave me skills and experience and confidence and prepared me for what lay ahead.

Chapter 3: Hunting

HUNTING has always been a major element in my life. One of the reasons Dad moved to Oregon was for the hunting.

Dad hunted with a buddy—he didn't take me along until I was twelve years old. That was the year he and his buddy each got a deer on opening day, which had never happened before. They didn't want to use their tags so early in the season so they put the bucks in the trunk of the sedan without tagging them.

They were driving down a rickety road to the highway when they saw a guy changing a tire. In those days you stopped to help.

The three men got to talking.

"You boys been hunting?" the man asked.

"Yes."

"Get any?"

Dad and his buddy probably couldn't help being a little excited about their first-ever opening-day success so they said, "Yes."

"Can I look?" the man asked.

"Sure," they told him and proudly opened the trunk. There were the two untagged bucks.

"Sorry, boys, but I'm the game warden." He took the deer.

Dad and his buddy had to go to court. They were trying to feed their families and the loss of the deer was hard on them. The judge gave them back the deer, but kept their hunting licenses.

It was still early in the season so Dad came to me and asked if I wanted to go hunting. It was my first time deer hunting. I had shot a BB gun (I didn't get the .22 until the next summer), but never a deer rifle. In those days, without a license Dad was not allowed to carry a rifle so I carried his .30-40 Krag[5] very early, bolt action

---

[5]The .30-40 Krag (also called .30 U.S., .30 Army, or .30 Government) was a cartridge developed in the early 1890s to provide the U.S. armed forces with a smokeless powder cartridge suited for use with modern small-bore repeating rifles to be selected in the 1892 small arm trials. Since the cartridge it was replacing was the .45-70 Government, the round was considered small-bore at the time. The design selected was ultimately the Krag-Jørgensen, formally adopted as the M1892 Springfield. http://en.wikipedia.org/wiki/.30-40_Krag

military rifle with a scope he'd stuck on. When we got to the site where Dad wanted to hunt, I put the rifle up on the limb of a brush pile and aimed where Dad said he had seen a buck. The rifle was too big for me. I had to hold it out at arm's length and I still couldn't see through the scope.

"Do you want me to shoot it for you?" Dad asked.

"No, I'll do it myself."

The buck could tell we were there and he was nervous. He had two options: run away through the brush or jump. He jumped. I broke his back with my very first shot of a deer rifle.

My dad said, "You lucky shit."

Over the years Dad continued to hunt, but never killed another deer.

I've made the same 'lucky' shot numerous times since then. My dad wasn't a good shot and nobody taught me how to hunt. It was a long time before I learned why I could make the shots I did. The way a mature buck functions, he'll generally lay against a hill facing downhill with his backside to the brush and his legs tucked under his body. When he gets a danger signal, whatever that may be, the buck instantly positions his feet under the middle part of his body and he does not stand up, he springs up. If you look at his bed, you will see four hoof prints in the middle of the bed. When his back became visible, I would break it with the first shot.

I did this over and over again. I'll explain why later.

My best friend in school, Ray, was a year older than me and very smart; he just missed being valedictorian of his class. Between his junior and senior year Ray got a job on a ranch in Lakeview east of Klamath Falls near the California border. All the hay was meadow hay from the upper end of the natural lake. It was a unique cattle ranch; they didn't use any motors, they used only horses and wagons to cut, rake and haul the hay.

The ranch manager took a liking to Ray.

In the fall he told him, "If you want to come over duck hunting, you can stay in the bunkhouse. Bring a friend if you want to."

Ray invited me to go duck hunting with him. I was a junior and playing football and would have to miss a week of practice and a game. I went to Coach and told him I wanted to take this trip. He said fine. I didn't bother to ask the teachers about taking a week off of school—my girlfriend, Sandy, would be there to get my homework.

Ray and I took off early Saturday morning and started hunting ducks and geese. The weather was nice, but that made it harder to get a shot because the birds were moving back and forth and flying high. In the fields there were these small, shallow lakes like puddles. Usually, we didn't leave our blinds until after dark so we could have the full daylight to hunt.

One evening, after not doing well all day, we headed back to the bunkhouse after the sun set. The moon was up. The ducks saw the moon reflection on one of the big water puddles and zoomed in on it. We could see where the ducks disturbed the water and shot into the disturbed area. Because of the shallow water, we could wade out and pick up the ones we hit. After that we had a bag full of ducks every night.

While we were there, Ray's dad and little brother wanted to come up for the last weekend of deer season when it was legal to shoot both doe and buck.

Ray was a dresser and liked to look good. Ray's dad was a mill manager and made good money, but he was careful with it. Ray had asked his dad if he would buy him this overcoat that Ray had his heart set on. It cost $25 (about $215 today). His dad had said, "No, you've already got your school clothes. You've got all you need."

Until then, Ray had never got a deer. When he came up to go deer hunting, Ray's dad said, "Ray, do you still want that overcoat?"

"Yeah."

"If you get a deer, I'll get you that overcoat."

Ray took me aside, "Ken, if you see an extra deer, will you shoot it for me? I really want that overcoat."

"Sure," I said.

The ranchers told us a good, timbered place to hunt and the four of us went out. I was in the center, Ray was on one side of me, and his dad and little brother were on the other side. We were spread forty to fifty yards apart walking up the timbered hillside and hoping one of us would scare up a deer. I saw a doe, threw up my rifle and shot her. I hadn't seen the buck behind her. When he jumped up, I shot him, too. I could hear Ray's dad and brother coming toward us—they'd heard the shots. I thought quickly.

"Ray, look, there's the doe you shot! I'm going over there to my buck."

"What?" He looked confused for a moment. "Oh, yeah, that's right."

He'd forgotten about asking me to cover for him, but recovered in time. He got his coat.

One day, just out of high school, I got up early and was out on Green Springs Road. For some reason, somebody had given me a real coonskin cap. I thought it was pretty neat so I wore it hunting that day. I was on the top of this draw looking down the slope. The temperature was pretty warm and I was getting sleepy. I had the gun lying across my lap and dozed off; my head fell forward. From the air, you could only see the cap, not my head. This big eagle dove on the cap. I woke up just in time and looked up. The compression from the air of the eagle's wings hit me in the face. If he'd hit, he would have sunk his talons into my head. My guardian angel was looking out for me.

Then I heard this screaming noise like I'd never heard before. I was still fuzzy from sleep and couldn't make it out, so I went over the ridge to see what it was. The animal either heard me coming or heard the eagle and we met on the ridge. I threw up my gun and shot it. At first, I figured it was a big bobcat, but it was probably one of the last lynxes in Oregon. When I picked him up, I put his forepaws over my shoulder, his head lay on top my coon skin cap, and his back feet touched just above my ankles. I gave the carcass to a school chum, Woody Brock, who did taxidermy on the side. We were going to get together and prepare the hide for tanning, but we didn't get to it soon enough and it spoiled.

The summer after I graduated high school my best friend, Ray, who was already in college, and I wanted to take a guy I worked with on his first deer hunt. Bill was three years older than me and had never hunted, but wanted to learn. John, a classmate of Ray's, came with us. We took Bill to the big rim rock up the Green Springs Road and out the Copco Road east of Ashland where I had shot my first deer. John and Bill worked the top of the rim rocks, and Ray and I worked the lower, patchy brush area. I loaned my hunting rifle to Bill and was carrying an older 30/30 lever action I borrowed from a friend. I was approaching a little patch of brush when, all of a sudden, on the far side of the brush, a buck sprung from his bed. I didn't see him, but can remember every split second: I heard antlers rattling in the brush—this meant his horns were hitting brush as he went up. I threw up my gun at the sound and in that split second saw his horns and shot.

Ray called out, "Did you get one?"

"Yeah, I got a nice buck," I yelled back. But wait, how did I know this? I never consciously saw a buck. My knowledge told me the horns came up, what they looked like, and exactly where I hit the deer, but I had no conscious picture of it in my brain. This wasn't a case of good eye sight; it was what I think of as subliminal perception.

That December there was a big storm and the ducks moved into these huge grain fields in Klamath Basin. The four of us—Ray, John, Bill and I—went hunting together again. Between each field was a frozen irrigation canal. Ray and John went one way and Bill and I went the other. The canal was elevated above the fields in a trough and way down there was a black spot on the ice and snow. Every once in a while we could see something moving. I came to the conclusion it were ducks. I told Bill, "Let's get down in the field where we can come up on them without them seeing us. When we hear them, we'll know we're pretty close to the middle of that black spot."

Bill had never shot a shot gun; he was very green as a hunter. My plan was to blast the ducks enmass—I wanted to get a lot of them. We climbed up the back of the grassy slope to the canal. We couldn't see them yet, but some of the ducks must have gotten nervous and flew up. Bill shot at one of the ducks that rose above the canal. That sent off the rest of them. I shot into the black mass. This created a hole. I shot into the mass again. We got twenty-two green head mallard males and three pintail males. No females. It was freezing cold and we had heavy rain gear on. The dead ducks were floating in the one open spot of water in the frozen canal.

"How the hell are we going to get all these ducks?" I asked.

Bill took off all of his clothes and dove into the freezing cold water and started tossing ducks back up to me. He got them all. We picked the feathers instead of skinning them; there was a three-eighths-inch layer of fat over the whole body from eating in the grain fields. I'd never seen ducks so fat. They were delicious.

I liked hunting the Green Springs road from Ashland to Klamath Falls. I was twenty and back living in my folk's house after I came back from working in southern California for a company called Croft & Neville, the site of another important spiritual message and where I made my first professional dives.

It was opening day of deer season and my friend Keith Wilson and I went up the slopes where I'd had good luck before. (Keith was my second partner in a log salvage business and remains a good friend.) Keith was hunting just down the hill from me a little bit. There was an oak thicket in a draw with some tall grass as you come out of the oak trees. I looked around and saw a nice set of horns sticking out of the two-foot grass. I put the sights of my .30-40 Krag[6] where I thought the buck's head was and pulled the trigger. The antlers fell over. Three other smaller bucks jumped up. One went up to the left—I shot him. I threw in a bullet. One went off the right—I shot him. I threw in another bullet and shot at the one going down the bottom of the draw, but didn't see that one go down.

Keith came running,

"Did you get any?" he asked.

"Yeah, I think I got four: one big one and three little ones."

We went down the draw and found that I had gotten the third little buck. I sent Keith up the hill to get one of the other little ones and I went up to get the other one. We got all three little bucks together to clean them out.

Keith said, "I thought you said you had four?"

"Oh, yeah." I'd forgotten about the first big buck.

We went back to the spot; he was lying right where I had shot him. I laid my rifle down in the brush, put one hand on his horns, a knee on his neck, and a knife to his neck to bleed him out. When the knife point went into his neck, the deer went straight up in the air. I went up with him and fell on my back. I had to pick myself up, get my gun from the brush, and take him down again. The first shot had grazed his neck and only put him to sleep. We dragged all four deer down the dry grass to the truck.

"What are we going to do?" Keith asked. "We only have two tags."

"Well, four illegal deer are as bad as two illegal deer."

We needed to keep a low profile so we hung the skinned and gutted deer up in the old fruit house behind my house. No one would see them there. Keith and I decided to let them hang to age. Our mistake was that there was no air moving in

---

[6] Ken: I bought this gun for $35 from a friend of Uncle Blackie's when I was working in southern California. The guns were ex-military and you could buy them cheap. I still have it. I think my brother Norman has dad's old Krag.

the fruit house. When we went to cut up the deer, there was mold on the carcasses. We didn't want to waste all that meat so we got some vinegar and washed it down. We decided to strip off all the meat from the bones to reduce the volume, take the prime stuff to make steaks, and make the rest into hamburger using an old hand grinder we had. We started in and we cut and we ground and we cut and we ground. Keith had brought a girlfriend. I was married by this time and my wife Sandy was there, too. The four of us went to work. When the sun came up, Keith, his girlfriend, Sandy and I were still grinding hamburger. We fried some up for breakfast. The meat was sour.

Earlier that fall, a friend in the produce business had bought a whole field of large yellow onions. He needed to store them until the price came up and I offered to let him use the old pens on our property the former owners had used to commercially raise chickens. He told me in return to use as many onions as I needed. It sounded good, but the onions were so hot you couldn't eat them on a sandwich, but fried with the sour deer meat, they both tasted better. Between Keith's family and mine we ate all the meat from those four deer; it got a little old having sour deer and onion twice a day, but it got us by another year.

A few years later, Keith and I were on a diving job on the Klamath River. We had to make a dive on Copco dam, two miles across the border in California, to clean out the debris that got in front of the trash gates.

It was a week or so before deer season. At the end of work one day I told Keith, "If we go to Copco Road, we might see a deer. That's where I used to hunt when I was a kid. I'd like to show you that country. You stay with your folks and I'll stay with Sandy's folks." Ashland was close by and we could stay with family before driving back three hundred miles to the Portland area where we lived.

We put our dive gear in the trunk of my Volvo sedan. It was an old car and the battery was always dead and the tank out of gas; I can't remember how many times we pushed it to get it going. As we drove, we saw a couple of does about fifty to eighty feet from the road. I parked the car and Keith and I walked around behind the car. Without thinking about it, I looked down and there was a rock on the side of the road. It was shaped like a small rectangular box, about two-and-a-half inches by an inch-and-a-quarter. I sensed there was something special about that rock. I didn't have a plan, but as I picked up the rock, one of the does raised her head to see what was going on. Without thinking, I reared back and threw the rock and broke the doe's neck. It was the only rock I ever threw at a deer. We gutted it out with a dull diving knife, put the carcass on top of the dive gear in the trunk, covered it up, and took it to Keith's family. They still had a couple of kids living at home; we were all struggling then and the extra meat helped.

Later, after I bought Sportcraft Landing moorage and my parents had moved back from Southern California to manage the marina, my dad and I went deer hunting on the east side of Mt. Hood. We parked the rig and my brother Norm took off down the hillside into the pine forest. Dad went with me. The loggers had moved some brush into piles for burning later. We didn't know it, but there was a big buck lying on the other side of the brush pile near us. The buck sensed us and sprang from his bed. Without thinking, I shot and broke his back. We gutted it out and then heard Norm shoot down below. Dad and I dragged my buck back to the van; Norm came up and helped us load it—he had heard our shot just before he made his shot.

"Norm, did you get one?" we asked.

"No," he said.

He told us he'd shot at a smaller three-point buck, but missed.

"What did he do after you shot at him?"

"He ran down the hill, but he didn't seem very nervous."

He was probably a partner of the big buck. A young buck often follows a mature buck and he may not have known the big buck was no longer alive.

We followed the trail and Norm scared up the little buck again and it ran down the hill to this little V where the brush was heavier. If the buck made it to the brush, we were going to lose him. Dad didn't even throw up his gun. I threw up my gun and took a flying shot just before the buck got to the V.

"Did you get him?" Dad called.

"I don't know. It was a pretty wild shot."

We went down to look and there he was—a nice little three point buck. We gutted it out and got ready to drag it back to the truck when I noticed that there was no blood and no holes in the hide. I thought, *Weird. How come he's dead and no blood?* I had to figure out how he died. Maybe I grazed his head, but I didn't see anything. Then I glanced in his ear and there was a glob of blood there. I rolled his head over and shook his horn to see if his skull was broken by the bullet. Nothing. I looked in the other ear. There was a little glob of blood there. The bullet went in one ear and out the other. The bullet didn't hit anything so it didn't expand and stop.

I don't believe I made those shots on my own. By this time in my life, I believed I had a strong spiritual connection and could ask questions. When I asked the spiritual, *How can I do these things?* The voice said, "What did you do with the meat?"

Now I understood. Early on, I got more than my share of deer, which helped feed my family, my friends, and their families. When I looked back, this connection became more obvious. Dad would have called me a lucky shit, but I believe that these were spiritually-guided kills that helped me to feed people who needed the meat. I know now that I was a puppet—I was used to feed others.

Some people have a hard time seeing it this way. A friend of mine says he knows people who make incredible trick shots and does not see what I did as anything that unusual. Other people think I simply have incredible eye sight. I used to belong to a gun club and I was only an average shot. I am so-so at pheasant and duck hunting. I am an OK shot at elk, but I consistently hit deer and kill them instantly—they are not wounded or crippled. I call these shots subliminal shots; I am not aiming at the animal in the traditional sense and am sometimes not even aware of the animal's presence until I take the shot.

With deer, I was consistently led to where the deer was bedded down, not near him or to the outside, but situated so the deer was right in front of me when it jumped up. Almost all of the shots went through the heart, lungs, or backbone; the big buck I stunned when hunting with Keith and the shot that went in one ear and out the other were rare exceptions.

A shot with a powerful rifle at close range in the heart, lungs or backbone kills instantly; the shot can only be made when facing the target, not swinging at an animal escaping to the side of the shooter.

The big thing is that I consistently walked straight to the deer. They didn't jump up from the side or run this way or that way; I don't think you can make the subliminal shot that way—the shot has to be made straight on. I was led to the deer so I could make a straight-on shot and get the deer. When hunting with a group, even when someone else decided who hunted where, I was the one who always walked right to the bedded-down buck; I was led directly to him and I consistently made fatal shots. I was often the only person in the group to kill a deer or even see one.

This sequence of events when hunting deer happened many times. What are the mathematical chances of that happening? It is my firm belief that I was spiritually led to these deer so that I could provide food for others.

Saying that makes me think of shots I missed and there is one incident that's kind of interesting. It was my first year out of high school and I'd gone by myself to an area I liked. When I got to a small ridge, I sat down to rest on a low-cut stump with my knees bent up. I was taking a breather, and this beautiful buck walked along the ridge. He stopped in total plain sight, 60-70 yards from me, a real easy shot. I put the gun on my knees, braced it, put him in my sights, and shot. An easy shot. The deer just walked away. What happened?

The next weekend, my friend Harvey, who had never shot a deer, and I went to the same spot. I said, "I got a shot at him last weekend, but didn't get him. Do you want to go look for him?"

Harvey took the far ridge and we both simultaneously went down. I heard Harvey shoot. He came running to me, "I got one, I got one!"

"Did you gut him out?" I asked.

He was too excited. We went back and it was the same buck I'd seen the previous week. Harvey was the oldest of six children and this was the first deer he'd gotten. It was great.

There is an elk head on the wall at my cabin in Halfway; we call this "Eric's elk." My son, Eric, and my brother, Norm, were

Ken Dye and Fred Weiler hunting elk near Halfway, Oregon (date unknown)

hunting on side-by-side draws. My youngest son, Chris, and I were going to push the elk up to them. I'd just crossed the border fence and there was a lot of timber ahead of me. Chris was down below me when we heard a shot. Then we heard another shot. I saw an elk running across the side hill above me through heavy timber. Norm had shot him in the foot and Eric had shot him in the stomach. Even with a bloody stump and a gut wound, the elk was running as hard as he could. I could see flashes of him through the pine trees, put the trees were spaced too tight together to get a shot. I found a spot between two big pine trees and swung my gun towards the opening. When I could see hair, I shot at the elk and got him in the heart. In my opinion, the elk would have died of his wounds, but could have run too far for Norm and Eric to find him. I wasn't as good a shot with elk as with deer, but the shot I made that time, I believe, was given to me so the elk would not suffer.

As I said before, at age nine I assumed everyone heard voices. Later I learned that people who heard voices were crazy, so for a long time I couldn't tell anyone about the voice or my feeling that I could not have made those shots alone. When I needed them, they were there.

If I could give a gift, it would be to give someone this spiritual connection. We are not alone. In this book, I'm doing my best to give everyone the message that having a spiritual connection is good and it's necessary to living a good life.

When I was young, I shot most everything; that's what we did then. Now hunting is not as important to me. Back then, shooting animals was fun and I was good at it. I had a change of heart when one of my sons, Mike, and I went hunting in Halfway, Oregon, where I built a log cabin. Like the rest of the kids, Mike went to Halfway with us as a little kid, but didn't participate in hunting. When he was in his late twenties and married to Jennifer, he said he'd like to go hunting, and bought a license and an elk tag.

The three of us—Mike, Jennifer and I—were walking down a skid road when I told him, "A lot of times a bull elk will lie down on this ridge."

It was the middle of the day, and that's when the elk are there. Sure enough, there was a big bull. The elk stood up. I had loaned my deer rifle to Mike and was carrying my dad's old .30-40 Krag. The bull was standing broadside to us, an easy target. I waited for Mike to shoot... And I waited... He didn't raise his gun. Finally, the elk started to move and I pulled the trigger on the Krag. Click.

Nothing happened. I'd never had a misfire before.

When I got over my surprise, I asked Mike, "Why didn't you shoot him?"

"Well, Dad, I just didn't want to kill him."

That was okay—Mike wasn't there to kill elk. He just wanted to experience elk hunting.

This was my first misfire and it caused me to reflect. Perhaps the gun misfired because it hadn't been used or oiled for a while. Or, perhaps, it was the spirit world giving me time to think about what Mike had told me. I'm glad the Krag misfired. If the gun had gone off, Mike's message to me would have been lost. Because of what he told me, I could take time to understand his position—our families didn't need the meat, so it wasn't necessary for me to kill the elk. Since then, I have hunted less and less.

One year my second wife Kathy, Mike's mother, and I were hunting on a heavily-rutted road near Halfway. I'd already used my elk tag, so was carrying my .22 and Kathy was carrying her elk gun. I looked up the road and this big blue grouse came out of the brush.

The blue grouse is a big bird, about a foot tall, and as big as a chicken. I took my .22 and took aim to shoot it—they are the best-tasting bird—when I thought, *If I shoot it, I've got to carry it all the way back to the truck, then I've got to take it home, clean it, and cook it.*

The grouse was standing on top of the next rut over from me, an easy shot, but I decided it was too much trouble to shoot him.

He was so pretty that I started talking to him. I was just talking to the bird in a calm, gentle voice, telling him what a good bird he was, and slowly walking toward him. I could see he was interested. He stood there until I could have reached out and touched him, but I didn't want to scare him, so I continued, instead, to walk up the road. The bird decided to walk with us. He'd walk a little way, cock his head to listen, and then walk on a little way. After thirty or forty yards he decided he'd gone far enough and went back down into the brush. I haven't shot a grouse since.

However, I still enjoy collecting guns; many I received as gifts or people gave them to me to store and then they passed on.

For example, there was my old friend Don Furre from Gladstone. His grandfather or great grandfather was a pioneer from Norway who came to America as a shipwright. Before catching the train to Oregon, he went to the armory in Springfield, Massachusetts, and bought a new Maynard[7] and four packages of shells. The grandfather built a home in Canby. He wasn't a hunter, so he put the rifle in the closet. The only time Don saw the gun fired was one day when a goose landed in a water trough—Don's dad took the rifle and shot through the side of the log trough, killing the goose.

For years Don told me about this gun. When his diabetes was getting to him, Don brought the gun to me and said, "Ken, this is the gun I want to give you. But there is one condition: I never want you to sell it."

I didn't to make a promise I couldn't keep so I said, "Don, I've got a lot of guns. I've never sold one."

His eyes lit up.

The gun is in great shape. After Don died, I showed the rifle to a collector. Then I told him about the shells.

"Ken, the gun is valuable," he said, "but the shells are really rare."

The shells were hand wrapped in packages of ten—five and five in opposite directions—in plain brown paper tied with twine. I keep them wrapped up in paper towels in a cigar box. The original paper wrappings are pristine. I also have some of the spent shells and slugs, and the paper wrap and twine from the open

Maynard rifle given to Ken by his friend Don Furre (photo 2013)

---

[7] Edward Maynard was born in Madison, New York, on April 26, 1813. In 1831 he entered the United States Military Academy at West Point but resigned after only a semester due to ill health and became a dentist in 1835... Maynard invented many dental methods and instruments, but is most famous for his firearms inventions. He achieved lucrative fame for his first patent, an 1845 priming system which cycled a small mercury fulminate charge to the nipple of a percussion cap firearm. Maynard's system used a magazine from which a paper roll, not unlike modern cap guns, advanced a charge over the nipple as the gun was cocked. Theoretically this accelerated a gun's rate of fire as the shooter could concentrate on loading and firing the gun. The system was quickly adopted by several commercial gun makers. http://en.wikipedia.org/wiki/Edward_Maynard

packages. Two of the original packages are unopened. My plan is to build a black walnut case and find a safe, suitable location to display it, maybe in the museum in Halfway.

Speaking of guns. It seems that every week or so there is a news story about someone going berserk and shooting a bunch of people and/or himself. The authorities want to solve the problem by eliminating guns. My friends and I have always had guns. A news reporter could make my collection look bad on TV, but having a lot of guns does not make you want to kill people.

Chapter 4: Learning to Defend Myself

WE ORIGINALLY moved from southern California to Oregon to be near my mother's family. My grandfather, Carl (Bud) Baker, had retired from the Long Beach, California, Police Department and moved to Ashland, Oregon. His old Long Beach precinct was on the waterfront. Bud's patrol covered a big pike—a carnival—and it was a rough area. Besides being the number-two motorcycle cop in the precinct, my grandfather was a professional boxer. The precinct had a gymnasium where the officers could work out.

Carl (Bud) Baker

The gym included a boxing ring. None of the other cops would fight Bud, so his fellow officers would tell a tough guy on the pike they had a cop for him to fight, then they would radio Bud, "We got a hot one," and everyone would come down to the gym while Bud worked the guy over. Grandpa was a quiet man. He never told me these stories; I heard them from one of the guys he worked with.

After he retired and moved to Oregon, Grandpa started a boxing club through the Kiwanis in Ashland. When we were in grade school and junior high, he taught me and my brother Norman how to box.

When I was a senior, our high school wanted to have a smoker (an informal boxing match). Grandpa had moved back to southern California. Our school did not have a boxing program, but the Pal Club in Medford trained kids to box and they sent their star fighter, a runner up in the Golden Gloves tournament championship.

I had not fought outside of Gramp's little club.

Most of the smoker was just kids duking it out for the fun of it. My fight with the fighter from Medford was the main event. This guy had silks with his name on it, boxing shoes, and a second—someone in his corner to put in his mouth guard, swab blood off his face, give encouragement, and so on. When the referee saw me in my plain shorts and tennis shoes, he said, "Ken, you can't fight this guy. He was the second runner up at State last year. You don't have the experience."

The ref called around looking for another fighter. There was no one. This was getting me psyched out; my legs were numb. I was scared, but willing to go on with the fight.

One of the coaches came by and asked, "Ken, do you know anything about this guy?"

"No," I answered.

"I watched him fight at one of the golden gloves tournaments," the coach said, "but he's not a true boxer. He has a brawler style."

This was great. I liked brawler style and knew a brawler couldn't fight against a trained boxer. We stood up, touched gloves, went to our corners, and waited for the bell. I decided I was going to have some fun. The bell rang. As we approached and met in the middle of the ring, I watched his eyes and hands. His were up and loose, but not defensive. Mine were similar, but in a boxer stance and closer to a defensive stance. I timed it perfectly and hit him with a left jab as hard as I could right to the nose. It staggered him. The fight hadn't really started yet. Now the brawler part of this guy was pissed. He was swinging and I was boxing. I had him against the ropes and he was hurt. I backed off and smiled. I knew I could knock him out, but let him throw wild punches while I racked up points.

To give him due credit, I had to fight every second. By the third round I was getting tired. It was spring and I hadn't worked out since football season the previous fall. My defenses slowed down and he clipped me with a left hook; he was left handed and it made my eyes roll. Today, a ref will call a standing eight count and, if you are okay after eight seconds, the fight can continue. But in those days being stunned was the same as being out while standing on your feet. I had been having fun with him, but ended up losing the fight.

One of the judges was a local coach. He came up to me after the fight.

"Ken, you had seventy-five percent of the points in this fight."

"I know," was all I could say. Good thing Grandpa wasn't there. He would have called me a dumb shit for not taking the guy down when I had the advantage.

It was a good experience. I never boxed again. I was in high school, but I was married with a baby. I had other business to attend to.

I didn't box again, but did get into situations that could have been fights if they had gone on longer. I bought my first little house, on Jersey Street in Gladstone, when I was doing log salvage. There was a guy the same age as me on Hereford Street named Fred Weiler. One evening in the summer I walked up to see Fred and he wasn't home, but his wife, Sherry, was there. She poured me a cup of coffee and we sat on the front porch. We had been having a lot of trouble with speeders on Hereford Street; in one year two little kids were hit by speeding cars. They weren't killed, but, even so, we were trying hard to get the traffic settled down. It was always on our minds.

As we sat on the porch a 1956 Chevrolet wagon came screaming around the corner right in front of us. It was going way too fast. I heard it coming and the anger inside me came up—I just went nuts. I grabbed my coffee cup—a big heavy mug—and was going to throw it through the windshield. However, I knew I couldn't really do that, so, instead, I threw the mug under the car. It rattled loudly and the driver stopped the car.

Inside the car were three young guys. The bigger and older of the three, around 24 years old, was driving. I told him our concerns about speeding. He was taking it pretty well when one of the passengers, his younger brother who was home on leave from Nam, jumped out the passenger side door and came storming around the back end of the car. I stepped back. As he came toward me, I watched his eyes. It's hard to explain, but I could look at his eyes and read what he had in mind, and I could see he was going to hammer me. I could also see he was calculating his steps so he could hit me. Just before he took that last step toward me, I took a half step toward him and that interrupted his mental calculations—he didn't know it yet, but I did. I didn't want to hurt him, so I threw my weaker left hand upwards towards his nose—he was taller than me—but, as I did it, I received a knowledge message to pull my punch so I wouldn't hurt him.

I hit him in the nose with the heel of my left hand; it wasn't a full punch. He didn't go down, but it shook him up. His eyes watered and it messed up his thinking. I reached up with my left hand and grabbed his hair—it was just long enough to get a good grip—and pulled him towards me. As he stumbled towards me, I started walking him in a circle to keep him off balance.

His brother and the friend hopped out of the car, but hadn't seen what I'd done and couldn't see why the brother was having trouble. After about the third circle, I wondered, *What am I going to do with him? If I put him down, I'm going to have to fight the brother and the friend, too.*

Fortunately, Sherry had called the police; I was never so glad to hear sirens. That ended the fight. The next day Fred and I went over to the guys' house and explained the situation. The older brother was very nice about it. The younger brother didn't say anything, but we didn't have any more trouble with him.

I had been trained to box, not fight, and fighting is not boxing. However, I knew what to do and was able to do it. This happened other times, convincing me that the spirit world was there, guiding me to diffuse a bad situation without either of us getting badly hurt and with no long-lasting ill feelings.

Part 2: Becoming a Man

Sandy and Ken dressed up for their Junior prom, in the
same clothes they would wear for their wedding a few
months later. Ashland, Oregon (1956)

Chapter 5: First Logging Job

BETWEEN MY junior and senior year of high school (1956) I worked in a gas station after school. The station was on the highway that goes over the Siskiyou mountain range in southern Oregon.

I was seventeen and eager to get on with life.

A regular customer came into the station on a logging truck that he ran between northern California and Medford, Oregon.

I asked him if I could get a job logging.

"Sure, I'll take you with me," he offered.

I made sure the pumps were covered and went with him back to California.

I rode down to the site and talked to the boss of the small logging company about a job. He said, "Why don't you come down here Monday morning. You'll have to camp out. There's no place to stay."

I didn't tell him I was seventeen. I came home on the trucker's next run to Medford and went back down in my car, a 1939 Mercury sedan. Everyone else camped out in tents. I didn't have a tent, so I put up a cot next to the car and kept a food box on the back seat.

We were logging a burn area. I started out working with the boss on the landing loading logs using a jury-rigged system. The truck pulled between an A-frame—a basic method for picking up logs. On our best day, we loaded seventeen trucks.

Next, I worked with the fallers. They put me between the faller and the bucker with a tape measure. After the tree was felled, I used my axe to trim limbs, then I measured the log length for the bucker, and marked the tree by chopping out a small v with the axe. I had to make the marks and run back up the mountain before the next tree was felled. I got so exhausted running up and down that mountain!

On one trip up the mountain I climbed onto a large stump that overlooked the valley and the river. I'd never been so tired. I told myself, *Ken, this is no way for a human being to exist.* I swore to myself that never again would I work for someone else for more than six months unless I was buying his company. I never broke that promise.

After each shift I put on a swim suit and snorkel gear and dove the Klamath River looking at fish; I was teaching myself to dive.

In the fall I had to quit logging to be home for football practice. I was going into my senior year of high school and my friend Ray, the one with the coat I helped get, was starting college. Each fall we got a job in the pear cannery for three or four weeks.

There was a conveyor and a trough going into a shed. Our job was to spill pears into the trough at a certain rate. Eight women inside the shed sorted and graded the pears before they went to the canner. In order to get the rate proper, the cannery sent an electrician who installed a clock with just the second hand attached; we had to spill a box of pears every so many seconds.

It was hotter than hell. We were outside, where it was bad enough, but it was really brutal inside the shed where the women were working with their arms going four hours at a stretch in the heat; we all worked eight hours with only one break in the middle of the shift. The clock was plugged into an electrical outlet under the conveyor; the electricity for the clock ran off the same circuit as the conveyor. I got an idea: I found a nail and dropped it across the two terminals to the clock, which shorted out both the clock and the conveyor.

When the conveyor stopped, all the women started shouting, "Yea!"

Each time I did this, we got a ten minute break while they reset the switch to the conveyor. I did this a couple of times a day for several days in a row. No one ever did catch on. They probably thought the system was overloaded from the heat, but it was the peak of the season and they didn't have time to check into it and fix the problem.

Chapter 6: Sandy

DOING A MAN'S work and teaching myself to dive made me eager to get on with life.

I worked for the logging company all week, camped in the woods in my car, and drove home to Oregon on the weekends. All week I was a filthy black mess from working in a burn area. I was eager to get home, clean up, and see my girlfriend, Sandy.

I met Sandy when we were in Junior High. We went steady through high school; neither of us dated anyone else. Sandy was thin and pretty with medium-length blond hair. She was a good student with enough credits to graduate midyear. I had always kind of used her to help me get through school. That way I didn't have to study and could spend my time hunting, fishing, and playing sports. All through school Sandy protected me.

Part of the problem was that I didn't have much respect for teachers in high school. I liked them as people, but did not think they were qualified to teach. For example, in my sophomore year I went into the algebra class. The teacher was a good guy. The start of the first day of class he told us, "Open your book and do the problems on page 1."

I was good at math, but the instructions on page 1 didn't make sense; it wasn't logical to me. I took my book and paper up to the teacher's desk.

"Mr. C—, I don't understand."

He took the paper and did the problem for me. He didn't explain it. I had the answer to the problem, but didn't know what it meant or how to do it myself. He could do the problem, but he couldn't teach it. I eventually dropped the class and took another math class. Other teachers were similar. But the bottom line is, I just wasn't interested in school; I was good at boxing, football, and making out.

Sandy and I were young and pretty serious. One night, after working in the woods all week, I was making out with Sandy; seconds later the voice came to me and said, "She's pregnant."

Neither of us could have known for sure so soon, but soon we had proof.

One weekend when I was home from my logging job, Sandy told me she had missed her period. It was three weeks after the voice told me she was pregnant. We discussed our options. I said, "Okay. We gotta get married and we need to get married really quick, like next week. I'll take you home and you tell your mother that we've decided to get married. I'll go home and tell my mom that we're going to get married next week."

We were seventeen years old and had our senior year of high school to get through.

When I got home, Mom and Dad were in bed. I called into their room, "Mom, I need to talk with you."

She came out into the living room; she had a nightgown on. Mom rarely wore curlers; she didn't need them, she was so beautiful. Dad, of course, wasn't really interested. He was sleeping. It wasn't important to him; he could find out about it later.

"Mom," I said, "Sandy and I are going to get married next week."

"Is she pregnant?" she asked.

"I think so. She missed her period last week."

"What's Sandy going to tell Lois?" My parents and Sandy's parents were friends. Lois, Sandy's mom, was not the same woman as my mother and would not take the news of Sandy's pregnancy well, so Mom repeated, "What's Sandy going to tell Lois?"

"She's going to tell her that we want to get married next week."

"Is she going to tell her anything about being pregnant?"

I shook my head. My mom walked over to the telephone and dialed. I remember this so clearly: my mother dialing and saying, "Lois, isn't it wonderful? The kids want to get married right away. Let's get together tomorrow and plan a romantic Reno wedding."

Lois agreed and our mothers met the next day to organize it all.

Sandy's mom never knew. [8]

---

[8] Sandy says, "I fell in love with Ken when I was 12 years old. I sat in the background and let him do what he wanted to do. He was my life from then on. We were in the same class. I often came over to Ken's house and we'd sit together in the big arm chair. I just kind of followed him around while he did what he wanted to do. I did a lot of things with him and his family, such as going hunting; I wasn't a hunter, but learned to shoot a rifle.

When my mother told him about the baby, Dad probably said something like, "Oh, the dumb shit." He'd do that; call me a dumb shit when I did something stupid and a lucky shit when I killed a deer.

Six of us went to Reno: me, Sandy, my parents, Sandy's mom and Sandy's stepdad. (Bill was younger than Lois and a wonderful guy; we were close. Unfortunately, he died of cancer when he was thirty-eight. Sandy and her mother were close, but Lois was much more reserved than my mom or her friends and I was never really comfortable with her.)

We took two cars to Reno. After the brief ceremony, Mom and Dad got into their car with Sandy's folks and we all went to gamble; it was before gambling was legal in Oregon so for us it was a big deal. (I've taken a lot of risks in my life, but I don't like to gamble. For instance, years later when we were on the way to Lake Mead for a foam project, we stopped in Las Vegas. I gave my two employees, Connie and Larry, each $500 to go play. Connie and Larry went through their money in a couple of hours. My second wife, Kathy, and I put about $20 in the machines and quit. Money is too hard to come by to waste it gambling.)

After the wedding, our parents went home to Ashland and Sandy and I went to California to a resort called Clear Lake. It was summer and our motel room was on a beautiful lake. We also went to the coast. I was going to be a professional diver so had my snorkeling gear with me; even on my honeymoon I wanted to get into the water. Sandy sat on the beach and waited for me.

After a few days in California we came home and lived with my parents. We went back to school in the fall. Sandy had enough credits to graduate at midyear. After that, it was tough for me because Sandy had always helped me with my school work and now I had to finish out the year on my own. It was hard, but I did it.

Sandy says: "Ken always knew he was good looking and cared what his hair looked like. He spent more time in front of the mirror than I did. (With her hands, Sandy demonstrates how Ken combed his hair down over the tip of his nose, then, with a dramatic motion, swept it back into a ducktail.) I had to push him away from the mirror so I could get to it; he would have stayed there all day."

Sandy says: "My parents were okay with the marriage. They figured that we should get married because, if we didn't, I was going to get pregnant. They never knew I already was. We were underage and our parents signed for us to get married. We were married in a church in Reno. I wore a short white dress and we walked down the aisle with just our parents in attendance. However, they and the people at the church made it like a real wedding for us. (Later Sandy dyed her dress red and wore it.) It didn't feel strange to be getting married so young; we thought we were very adult and that we were supposed to be married.
  "We were the only ones of our friends who were married or had a baby—as a couple, we were kind of by ourselves. Ken still had his friends that he went hunting with. I went to the football games and watched him play and waited for him outside the dressing room when the game was over." (It sounds like a lonely life, but, even today, she says she liked being "Ken Dye's wife." She loved it.)

Otherwise, I was still living at home and going to school. Life hadn't changed that much for me.

As it turned out, Sandy and I weren't that compatible, but it wasn't obvious then.[9] Ours was the smallest Class A school in Oregon, with about six hundred high school students in grades nine through twelve. I had a large circle of friends. Sandy had a couple of close girlfriends. Our differences became even more apparent after we left school.

---

[9]Here is an interesting fact: In 1939, the year Ken & Sandy were born, Kenneth was the 13th most popular name given to boys and Sandra was the 13th most popular name given to girls. (Ken's first name is actually Wayne, like his father, but always went by the name Ken.) Perhaps they were fated to be together—and doomed to bad luck.
http://www.babycenter.com/popularBabyNames.htm?year=1939

Chapter 7: First Dive

AS SENIORS in high school (1956-57) we had to write occupational reports. Naturally enough, I wanted to do my report on professional diving, but a friend of mine, Hal Edick, was a year older than me and had done his report the year before on the same subject. Before moving to Ashland from California, Hal had made a few dives in the early '50s. He moved to Oregon before sport diving became popular or well known. Even with his experience, it was difficult for Hal to get information for his report.

We were supposed to do interviews, write letters and so on. I didn't know where to find a diver in Ashland to interview and I didn't want the teacher to think I was copying Hal's paper, so I didn't do the report. I wish I had.

I wrote about morticians instead. My father-in-law, Bill, was a mortician. He also had an ambulance service and responded to traffic wrecks. In my spare time, I worked in the funeral home, cleaning up and helping Bill with whatever he needed. Of course, there were a lot of dead bodies coming in and out. One evening, I was at the funeral home when my family doctor came in. He asked me, "Ken, have you ever seen an autopsy? Do you want to see one?"

"Sure."

A woman had died of cancer. As he was doing the autopsy, the doctor held up organs and showed me where the cancer had attacked the organ. It was gory, but I now had a lot of good material for a report. It was probably the only time I got an A without (direct) help from Sandy.

I didn't report on diving, but I did pursue diving. At the time, commercial diving was hard hat helmet diving in heavy suits. Scuba diving had been developed a few years earlier in WWII, but it was still new technology. Hal had a couple of tanks and regulators. The gear was new, but because the technology was also new, it was hay wired together without any of the modern safety equipment or harnesses we had later. Hal rigged the harness himself from belt buckles and scraps of leather. We had no thought of safety. (Note: Scuba was in its infancy in

1948 when Ken was in the fourth grade and heard the voice for the first time. In 1956 or 57, when Ken made his first dive, safety devices like buoyancy compensators were only in the experimental stage.)[10]

For my first dive, four of us drove up to a place called Lake of the Woods, a beautiful lake south of Crater Lake National Park: Hal Edick, who owned the equipment, my good friend and neighbor, Gee Hodges, who was dating Hal, and my wife Sandy.

We took the family car and arrived at the lake an hour later. The water was a clear, still blue; in places we could see the bottom. The gentle lapping of the waves on shore and a small animal chattering created a soft undertone.

We got out of the car and stretched.

Hal handed me a tank and weight belt. The weight belt was a conventional man's belt strung with lead weights and attached to the back of the tank. The harness has another belt attaching the tank to my body; neither belt had quick releases and the equipment was strapped to my body in such a way that I couldn't shed it if I wanted to. We didn't have wetsuits.

After I was rigged up, Hal put on his gear and picked up a spear gun; we were going to look for fish.

Hal said, "Follow me," and away we went.

We waded out to deep water. After we went down, I realized I was extremely heavy; I was plowing the bottom rather than hovering above it. Also, unbeknown to me, my tank was only half full of air.

We were a couple hundred yards from shore moving around looking for fish when it became harder and harder for me to breathe. Finally, I realized I was running out of air. I grabbed Hal, pointed to my regulator, and then pointed up. I headed to the surface, only a few feet over our heads, but I was carrying so much lead weight that it was tough going. When I finally reached the surface, the wind was blowing hard and waves washed over my head, making it difficult to draw a full breath. After working toward this day for half my life I nearly drowned in eight feet of water on my first dive.

---

[10] In 1957, F. G. Jensen and Willard F. Searle, Jr. began testing methods for manual and automatic buoyancy compensation for the United States Navy Experimental Diving Unit (NEDU). http://en.wikipedia.org/wiki/Buoyancy_compensator_(diving)#cite_note-NEDU57-11

Somehow I managed to get my head out of the water and take a deep breath. Hal surfaced next to me. He got behind me and unbuckled the gear. I dropped it and swam for shore; I figured he could drag his own gear back to shore.

Given what I've done since then, it would have been pretty embarrassing to die that way. That close call should have deterred me, but it only made me more determined to become a professional diver.

Chapter 8: Laurie

LAURIE WAS BORN in the Ashland community hospital on April 8, 1957. At that time, fathers did not go into the delivery room with their wives. I was eighteen and in high school. No way did I want to go in there! I don't think I'd go into a delivery room today. Mom and Dad were at home when Sandy and I went to the hospital. I sat in the waiting area while the doctor took care of Sandy.

When Sandy was in the delivery room and starting contractions, our family doctor came out and said, "Ken, don't plan on taking the baby home right away."

"Why not?" I asked.

"The baby needs to be five pounds to go home" he explained. Sandy looked small and the doctor assumed the baby was small, too.

Off the waiting area was a hallway. The delivery room was on my side of the hall, and the recovery rooms were on the other side of the hall. I waited in the hallway for a long, long time, not knowing what to do. I could hear Sandy screaming during delivery and swore we'd never have another baby.

At last, a door burst open and the doctor came to talk to me; he was holding the baby in his arms.

"The baby is doing fine," he said. As it turned out, Sandy only looked small because she wasn't carrying much fluid. Laurie was 7 pounds 14 ounces.

That's what I needed to hear. He went on to say, "This birth was difficult for Sandy. She's not built for having children. The shoulder came first and it tore Sandy pretty bad."

Not having any more kids was fine with me.

When I first saw Laurie I was shocked. Because of the tight birth canal, her head was pointed and there was blood everywhere. My first impression of Laurie was of a bloody, screaming little monster with a deformed head.

I was young and didn't know anything about children or childbirth; no one had taken me aside or warned me of any of this. I'm not sure how much Sandy knew, but I thought all babies were beautiful. I learned a lot of things through experience and this was an important lesson.

My mom could have told me about childbirth, but she had an easy time giving birth; she was made to have children. Sandy's experience was a big surprise to her, too.

I liked playing with the baby and would carry her up the stairs in the crook of one arm. It was Sandy's job to take care of her; I just liked to play with her. Sandy didn't want to nurse, but heard it was good for the baby. Plus, my mom had done it and expected Sandy to do it, too, so she nursed each of our kids for the first six weeks.

My high school friends were fine with the marriage.[11] Actually, not much changed for me. I still lived in the same house; I had my good old buddies; we still played football, hunted, and fished together. My friends were more interested in some Model T parts in a big building in the back yard, which I'd torn apart and thought about putting back together, than they were in my being a husband and father.

By the end of the school year, I had earned enough credits to graduate high school. Sandy and I graduated together with our parents and precious baby in the audience at the ceremony.

The next day, I waved goodbye to my parents. Sandy and I stood on the porch of the familiar pale yellow house with Laurie in my arms as Mom, Dad, and Norm drove off to California. After we had been in Oregon for nearly thirteen years, Dad's former boss, the big-time corporate attorney, had tracked us down and called from L.A. saying, "I'm going to build a new boat and I'd like to have you come back as the Skipper."

I was a high school student one day living with my parents, and the next day a husband and father paying rent. It was scary; I knew I had to get busy.

---

[11] Today Sandy says, "We never felt (too) young. Even at seventeen, being Ken's wife and the mother of his child felt like what I was supposed to be doing."

Chapter 9: Tunnel Job

THE FATHER of my best friend in high school was a sawmill manager. (Ray's dad was the one that promised to buy Ray the new coat he wanted if he got a deer that time we went hunting at the ranch.) Ray's dad gave me a job the same day my parents left for California. I appreciated the job and needed the work, but mill work was repetitious and boring: I stacked boards as they came off the planer chain. It drove me crazy and I quit after four days.

My fellow graduates were going to work, too. One of my friends went to work on a construction job building an irrigation tunnel through the mountains. I worked on that crew for six months and quit after Christmas. In that time I learned a lot of lessons:

One lesson was about working with men. This job involved a lot of hand work manually mucking gravel. This is where Bill, the guy I took on his first hunt, and I got to know each other. The day foreman was a laborer from Portland who didn't have any management skills. He was kind of a cocky little guy, but he could get away with it because he was the foreman. One day he tried his bullying tactics with me. Some minor issue came up and he jumped me about it in front of the crew. I stood up to him and showed him he was wrong and he backed off. After that, if there was any trouble with the boss the other guys would come to me knowing I wouldn't take any shit off the foreman.

Another lession was about working with officials. We had some equipment called dumpies—a yard-square steel box with three wheels and a small diesel engine used to haul broken rock and muck from the head of the tunnel to the opening. Like most equipment on this job, the dumpies weren't maintained well. The scrubbers on the diesel engines were broken and the dumpies filled the tunnel with smoke. The air mechanism to push out the smoke was always broken down, too—the air in the tunnel got so thick we couldn't see and we came out at the end of each day covered with diesel soot. (It seems that we should have come down with something, but since a lot of us went to school together, I have been able to follow up with several of these guys and none of us developed lung issues.)

One day I was driving one of the dumpies and had to take it to the shop for repairs. This was common. As I pulled up to the shop I saw a sedan pull up to the site with "State Industrial Accident" printed on the side. This was my chance to bring the poor conditions at the tunnel to the attention of someone who could do something about it! The car stopped near the shop. I kept the dumpy going pretty fast, then slammed the brakes on hard, but, like everything else, they were worn out and the dumpy slammed into the back of the shop.

The guy ran out and asked anxiously, "Are you okay?"

"Sure," I told him. "The brakes don't work and that's how we have to stop it."

The guy jumped in his car, took off, and I was thinking things were going to get better. Nothing changed. I figured he must have been bought off.

I also learned to handle explosives, which came in handy later. One of my jobs was to make up the shot—explosives with delay caps—for the miners. To make the tunnel, which was eight feet in diameter and almost a mile long, the miners bored a series of eight-foot-long holes in a circle pattern with several rings of holes leading to the center. They stuffed the holes with sticks of dynamite and primer cord tied together with delayed timing caps. The delayed caps would first blow out the center section, called the reliever, which allowed the other rock, such as the raisers, some space to go when it blew rather than blowing against solid rock. The miners blew the circle in sections. The rock would shatter and blow out a bit. Guys like Bill—whom we had nicknamed "Retriever" for the way he had gotten the ducks we shot out of the frozen irrigation canal—and I scooped up the rock with shovels and used the dumpies to haul the broken rock to the dump area.

The tunnel job taught me a lot. I learned about dynamite—by helping the miners load the holes and shoot them; I used dynamite later when I worked on the Ice Harbor Dam and to blow up a killer snag on the river. I learned that one can't always count on officials to do the right thing. And I learned to earn respect by standing up for myself and what I believed was right.

Chapter 10: Croft & Neville

I SAVED UP a few dollars working on the tunnel, which paid for our move to southern California where I could pursue my career in commercial diving. My first income tax refund was about two hundred dollars—I used it to buy a tank and regulator. I already had a mask, fins, and snorkel.

I had no skills when we moved to California. No occupation. I was just there, but I was willing to work wherever I was needed. I became depressed during this period because I couldn't get a good job, let alone a diving job. I worked at miscellaneous jobs, part-time stuff here and there. Sandy, Laurie and I were barely making it. Whenever I got a chance and on weekends, I hunted and went diving. We ate a lot of rabbit, abalone and fish. It's funny to think these are delicacies today. For us they were survival food.

I went to work for a time for my dad's older brother, Lloyd, in Huntington Beach. In those days (1958), oil fields had pools of oil from spills. The oil floated on top of water that collected in the pools. Uncle Lloyd, whom everyone called "Blackie Dye," had an oil vacuum business. It was dirty work, but Uncle Blackie was a lot of fun and people enjoyed being around him.

One day I told Uncle Blackie I was going to get into diving.

"I have a friend who goes sport diving all the time," he said. "I'll introduce you."

Leonard was the same age as my parents and had an industrial engine truck repair business. He was just getting into rebuilding ex-military compressors and converting them into systems for filling dive tanks. I told Leonard I was going into the dive business. We often went diving together to pick up abalone and stuff. When I returned to Oregon, Leonard wanted to stay in touch. I later bought a compressor from him for my first business. We stayed close until he died.

One of my part-time jobs in southern California was driving a truck three days a week. One day I had to deliver rebar and some equipment to a construction company on Pacific Coast Highway in Newport Beach. It was a fine day and I drove along the highway until I saw a small sign on the bay side of the road that read "Croft & Neville". I turned into the narrow alleyway and followed it to the warehouse. As I turned my truck into the alley, the voice once again came to me. It said, "You are going to work here."

It was only the third time I'd heard the voice, but it felt familiar and didn't worry me.

I pulled up to the shop and went in. A couple of young guys were standing just inside the delivery bay.

"I brought the stuff from the warehouse. Where do you want it?" I asked.

One of them nodded and said, "Just dump it alongside the road. Over there."

"Yeah, okay," I said. "Is the boss around?"

The other guy said, "He went down to pick up the mail. He'll be back soon." He pointed to the other end of the warehouse. "Go on into the office and wait for him there."

I stacked the Croft & Neville order by the side of the alley and went back to the office. No one was there. Except for a counter, the room was bare. I was on one side of the counter and opposite me, behind the counter, was a door to the outside. After a few minutes, a short guy about thirty-five years old came through the door. He had a bundle of mail in his left hand and was reading a letter he held in his right hand. He was involved in reading the mail and did not seem to notice me.

"Are you the boss?" I asked.

"Yep," he said. He glanced up and took me in, then looked back down at the letter.

I took a deep breath and said, "I'm looking for a job."

He looked up and smiled. Then he said, "Why don't you come to work on Monday morning at eight o'clock?"

"I'll be here," I promised. As I left the office, I wondered if the voice spoke to him, too; he didn't know a thing about me when he hired me.

Croft & Neville wasn't just any company. It was the right place to launch my career. They built wood docks for private homes along the bay, similar to the work my son Eric does today, except Eric builds docks out of steel. While I was at Croft & Neville I made three working dives; I cut pilings, retrieved anchors, surveyed launching ways, and cleared the launching ramps of debris. I joined the Carpenters

Union and two nights a week went to apprenticeship school. The company paid well, which was good for my family, and I was able to buy a wetsuit and more gear. It felt good to be starting my diving career.

The voice was absolutely right to lead me to this company.

Croft & Neville was a good company. My boss gave me opportunities to do different kinds of skilled work. Besides diving, I ran his tugs and built seawalls. I appreciated the company and loved the job, but soon my six months were up and I wanted to quit. The boss offered me year-round, fulltime work to stay. It was an honor—he only kept a couple guys year round.

"No," I said, "I'm moving back to Oregon in two weeks."

"What are you going to do in Oregon?"

I had thought a lot about this. I said, "I'm going to go into the salvage business and dive for sunken logs—all those sunken logs in the rivers and lakes of Oregon. I'm going to dive down, bring them up, and sell them."

No one else was doing that kind of work. At this time, I had made only three professional dives, but I felt I was ready.

He just shook his head and wished me well.

Two weeks later, Sandy and I packed our belongings in the back of our old 1948 Ford pickup truck and drove north to Ashland with Laurie. She was two years old and Sandy and I were twenty.

Part 3: The Log Salvage Business

Ken on log (April 24, 1963)
Source unknown. Clipping says: Basic for River Bottom
Loggers. Less than an hour's actual work went into recovering
the log shown above from the bottom of the Willamette River
and onto a slip, but it was tough while it lasted. Two former
Ashland High school classmates have set up an organization
to recover sinker logs from the river and so far have recovered
between 600,000 and 700,000 board feet of logs that
previously were thought to have been lost forever. They are
operating the only kind of salvage business of its type on the
river and are proud of the fact their operations are showing a
profit.s

Chapter 11: First Partnership

NEARLY A YEAR before Sandy, Laurie, and I moved to southern California, I met an older guy who was also interested in starting a log salvage business. Richard Smith was twenty-six or so and in his last year of college. Richard and a friend of his, who had a dive tank, had been hired by one of the mills to swim around a lake used to store logs to see what was in the bottom of the lake. The mill was going to donate the lake to the State of Oregon for a steelhead pond, but needed to know what was there first.

The lake was full of sunken logs and the State wanted them removed.

When Sandy and I got back from California, I looked Richard up. We immediately began thinking of ways to make a log salvage venture work. The mill's lake looked like a good place to start.

Although I had dive experience with Croft & Neville, I had never tried to salvage logs. I figured I needed to salvage some logs to know what I was talking about when I went to the mill manager. I invited a friend to go to Klamath Lake with me to an area where a saw mill had stored some logs. I put my dive gear into the truck and we drove the sixty miles to the lake. It was winter, but I wasn't concerned with the weather—I just wanted to get a choker around a log.

My friend, Charlie Gourley, and I went out to a peninsula that jutted into the lake. Logs were stored in a sheltered area and there was a little mill on the edge of the bay. We were sitting on the point when we saw a small steel pond boat with two guys in it heading to the log storage area. The water was about eight feet deep and murky. They were fishing for sunken logs to salvage, but it was elusive work because when they found a log, they had to poke it until they found the end. Then they dropped a choker cable around it, but, since they couldn't see the end of the log, they were trying to wrap the cable around the log blind. Once in a while they got lucky, snagged a log, and towed it to the mill. In this way they kept the log pond area from building up with sinkers.

This was the opportunity I had been wishing for. I watched the guys in the pond boat blindly snag logs a couple of times and decided to help them. I put on my dive gear and swam out to where they were working.

I hollered to them, "Give me the chokers. I'll hook them up and you guys tow."

"Oh yeah?" they called back. They must have wondered what a guy was doing out there with scuba gear on. "Okay."

They realized that this method would save them a lot of time and work. They threw the choker into the water; I grabbed it and immediately sank because it was so damn heavy. I went to the bottom, dragging the steel cable around, found a log, placed the cable over the end of the log, and handed the other end of the cable back to the guys in the boat. They gave me another choker to set while they were gone. Down I went.

Charlie was not a diver; he stood on the beach watching.

The two guys towed the first log to the mill and came back to me in the lake. Each time they took a log to the mill, I went down and choked another log. We did this several times until my air tank went dry. Before I swam away, I waved goodbye.

My pulse quickened. I had used my diving skills to salvage logs! I had done it. I was ready to go into business. I couldn't believe my luck. What were the odds the mill would be fishing for logs just when I turned up to dive for them? I was in the right place at the right time. Was I spiritually led? Or just a lucky shit, like my dad said? As time went on, there were too many instances like this for me to doubt there was something more to this than luck.

Chapter 12: Medco

IN 1959, Medco was the biggest mill in southern Oregon. The mill owned a lot of timberland above Prospect, toward Crater Lake. There was a manmade lake on the mountain used to store and sort logs until the mill was ready to process them; a railway ran from the lake down to the valley where the mill was located. The mill loaded the logs onto railroad cars and took them by rail down the mountain to the mill. For years and years, maybe decades, they used the lake to store and sort logs. Over the years, some of the logs sank.

This was the mill that hired Richard and his friend to dive the lake to see what was there before turning it over to the State for a steelhead pond.

At the time, I was working construction building houses. The weather that winter was really bad and the crew had a lot of time off. One day, when the weather kept us from building, I put on my best clothes—not much better than my work clothes, but cleaner—and drove to the Medco office in Medford. I asked the receptionist if the manager was around. She looked up and pointed in the right direction.

He was in his office.

I introduced myself and said, "I'm in the log salvage business." I stretched it just a bit—I choked logs that one day at Klamath Lake, but had not been paid for doing it.

I told the manager I was interested in salvaging the sunken logs in Medco Pond. "Are you interested in getting them out?" I asked him.

The manager was a casually-dressed man about thirty-five or forty years old. He said, "We'd like to get those logs out of there. How much would you charge?"

Well, I'd thought of this. I knew something about log scale. I told him I'd charge $12.00 per 1,000 board feet to deliver the logs to the beach. I also threw in a decimal C formula—a formula for scaling a log to determine its board feet that, along with log scale, I'd picked up while working the logging business in California when I was in high school; I figured it would give me some credibility. In reality I was twenty years old and winging it.

The mill manager said, "Well, the logs don't do us any good on the beach. I want them out of the lake and cold decked. If I can arrange for a D8 Cat, for the twelve bucks can you cold deck them for us?"

Cold decking meant bringing the logs out to a flat area and stacking them with the Cat so the logs could be loaded onto trucks.

I said, "We can do that for you."

He said, "I suppose you're a Cat operator, too?"

I said, "Oh, yeah." I was winging it again. I had set chokers behind a Cat, but that was it.

"When can you start this operation?" he asked. "We've got to get out of there before the State gets on us."

"Well, we've got to do some modifications to our equipment," I told him. I was winging it again to have time to put it all together; we didn't need to modify equipment, we needed to build it. This was January. "It'll probably be March before we can get started."

"That'll be fine. How about if we draw up a contract?"

I didn't realize what had happened until I got back in my truck and was headed home. Then I was amazed at my good fortune. Within fifteen minutes I had a contract. I had a business. I had a real diving job. It was incredible.

Now, I don't take any credit for that. There was no voice involved. I was physically there, but these things don't just happen without help. The mill manager didn't even check my credentials. He just said, "Let's do it. I'll draw up a contract and we'll start in March."

One or both of us had to be spiritually led.

I went back and met with Richard at his house and told him we had a contract. We started making plans. We needed money—it was a major problem. I was working construction, but was out of work most of the winter—I made just enough to pay the rent and feed my family. Richard also had a wife and a baby boy that was severely handicapped. His wife, Barbara, had a secretarial job; Richard had three months of college left and didn't work.

January through March 1960 were the busiest months of my life. I had to make good on my commitment to Medco and prove to myself I could do all the things I promised.

We needed to put together equipment. I did a little design of a pontoon barge. I had a cutting torch and borrowed a welder. Richard and I went to a steel company and said, "We're new in the log salvage business. We've got a contract with the Medco guys and we need to build steel pontoons."

The steel company guy said, "Yeah?"

I said, "The hitch is, we don't have any money, so we can't afford to hire a welder. Give us folded steel and we'll take it from there."

"You got a contract with Medco. That's good enough for me. You can pay us when you get paid."

What a break that was.

We used my partner's ski boat trailer to pick up the folded steel, unloaded it in my driveway, and started building a pontoon barge.

After the barge was built and painted, we needed some motors for it. At the time, most fishermen used a standard 25 horsepower Mercury motor. Jet pumps for outboards had just come out. A lot of fishermen were trading in their 25 horse Mercs for the larger outboards with jet pumps and the market for used Mercury motors was overloaded. We made a deal with an outboard motor dealer we knew to give us two motors and controls and promised to pay him when we could; he was happy to get rid of them.

Now we had a barge with two motors. Next, we needed a winch to crank up the logs. There was an unused log float at the lake where we were going to be working that had an old hand-cranked Beebe crab winch. We told ourselves, "We're sure Medco won't mind if we borrow that." So we got our winch.

Next, we needed a pair of logging tongs. When I was in high school and hunting on the Klamath River, I ran across a big, old pair of logging tongs lying in the brush alongside the river. For all I knew they were still there. One night my partner and I were sitting around having a beer, talking about what we still needed, and I remembered those old logging tongs. We hopped into Richard's car, a 1953 Chevrolet, with the rest of the six pack, and over the mountains we went; it was about sixty miles to the spot I'd seen the logging tongs. We had a flashlight and walked along the river and, sure enough, there they were. This was a big set of tongs, much bigger than we needed, but we couldn't afford to buy new ones. It was all we could do to carry them, but we got the huge set of tongs back to the car and into the trunk.

We needed tongs to pick up logs from the bottom of a lake or river. So we wouldn't have to swim around carrying heavy tongs, we dove holding a piece of cedar wood we had carved and wrapped with heavy twine attached to a screwdriver. We took turns diving and driving the barge. The diver hunted along the murky bottom looking for logs. When he found one, he shoved the sharp end of the screwdriver into a soft spot in the log and let the cedar plug float to the surface. The barge handler pulled up by the cedar float and released the tongs; the diver put the tongs over the log to be winched up to the barge where we both worked to secure the log alongside for hauling. This pair of tongs was much larger than we needed, but we didn't have any money so we had to use these. Later we got a lighter pair that worked better.

Richard and I ran into a mutual friend who sold trailer houses. He had a shabby trailer taken as a trade-in that he hadn't been able to sell. He said, "Ken, I'll rent it to you for $25 a month." I told him if he would deliver it to our lake site, we'd take it. Now we could live onsite on the cheap.

Lastly, we needed Medco's Cat and I needed to see if I knew how to start it. I

Charlie Gourley on the rickety old D8 Cat Medco gave Ken and Richard to use (1960)
Charlie was a neighborhood kid that worked for Crater Lake National Park as an equipment operator. We were friends. When he heard we had a Cat, he asked if he could come out and run it for us. He's the one that that rode with me over to Klamath Lake the first time I dove on a sunken log. That trip, in the middle of winter, was one of many events that were too much of a coincidence to deny a spiritual influence.

decided to stay in the trailer at the lake the night before Medco delivered the bulldozer. That way, I could catch the guy when he brought in the Cat and see what he did. I was sure once I got it started, I could run it. Pretty soon the truck pulled in and I ran out. The driver got out, ran the Cat off the back of the truck, shut it down, and left. It was pretty old and beat up, they weren't crazy enough to give us a new one. I jumped on the Cat before I forgot what I'd seen the driver do. The engine was still warm and it started right up. *Okay*, I thought, *I can run this thing. No problem.*

We transported the pontoon barge up to the lake piece by piece; the outboard motors, gas tanks, and the barge itself. The trailer house, winch, and tongs were already onsite. We borrowed the Beebe winch off the float and bolted it to the pontoon boat. I turned twenty-one on February sixth. We signed the Medco contract around February eighth or tenth.

We were in business.

A Douglas fir log normally does not sink; hemlock sinks, cedar sinks, and redwood sinks. At the Medco log pond (actually a lake), a couple of large fir logs were ninety-nine percent sunk. They weren't down quite all the way in the water, but were lying in the brush alongside the shore. We grabbed them and pushed them down the lake with the pontoon boat to a place where we could get hold of them with the Cat and pull them out. Once a large log is on flat land, it is easier to move by pushing it with the Cat than by pulling it. One of these logs was so big we couldn't move it. As it comes out of the water, a wet log feels heavier and heavier. For this log, one D8 Cat couldn't do it.

Medco had a yard a couple of miles down the road that was part of the same mill as the one we were working for. We told them we needed another Cat. The D8 is a large Caterpillar tractor.[12] With two of them we were able to drag the large log out of the lake; we used one Cat to push the log and one to pull it. As we skidded the log down the road, a cable broke and we had to repair it. The log was huge, eight feet or so in diameter with 7,740 board feet of lumber in it. It was the largest Douglas fir we ever salvaged.

Ken Dye, Richard Smith (at controls), Neil Knutson (on log) Medco Pond on the first barge Ken made. (Jan. 1961)

---

[12] D8 Caterpillar, Production 1935-2004, Length 186 in., Width 101 in., Height 84 in. Weight about 80,000 lbs depending upon year, model and accessories. Propulsion: tracks. http://en.wikipedia.org/wiki/Caterpillar_D8

By summer we had the logs out of the lake, delivered to shore, hooked to the Cat, dragged to a flat area, and stacked into a cold deck. We had fulfilled our contract.

Once we fulfilled the Medco contract, we got a second contract along the Oregon coast in Brookings salvaging logs for two small mills. We brought up redwood logs from the first pond and hemlock logs from of the second pond. We had given the old house trailer back to the guy we rented it from and three of us— my partner Richard, Neil, and I—were living in an apartment. Neil Knutson was a fun-loving guy going to college with Richard and was interested in everything, including diving, and occasionally helped us out with a little diving, but mostly we used him to run the hand winch. He had a beautiful wife who worked in a pharmacy in Ashland. Sandy and Laurie were also living in Ashland again in my parent's old house.

The three of us guys raised some hell and got kicked out of the apartment and had to camp out on the beach by the Pacific Ocean. One day, there was no food in the food box and I swam out and picked up the biggest abalone I'd ever seen. Today the shell sits on my coffee table.

Chapter 13: Boise Cascade

IN THE FALL Richard and I got a job with Boise Cascade Corporation at a place called Valsetz, in the Cascade Mountain range west of Salem.[13] Boise Cascade was a nationwide company and we were excited for the contract.

We bought a used Dodge flatbed truck to move our equipment. The truck was overloaded, making it an illegal load, so we moved everything from Brookings two hundred miles up to Valsetz in the middle of the night.

We had an agreement with the Boise manager to salvage the logs out of the lake. Some of the logs were very, very old. The lake was built during the beginning of World War I by damming the south fork of the Siletz River. One log we salvaged carried the Barefoot brand stamped on the end—the last year the Barefoot brand was used was 1917.

The manager told us he wanted us to start cleanup at the far end of the lake by the dam; the large plywood mill was at the other end of the lake. Once we brought the logs up from the lake bottom and towed them to the mill, the mill would pick out the logs, cold deck them, and then feed the logs directly into the mill. We'd pick up a log or two, and then have to run all the way up the lake to the mill with our little 25 horse outboards. It was kind of slim pickings by the dam; we figured we'd make our money when we got to the dump area where the main logs were located. For a month or so we picked up logs by the dam, not making much money; we were just barely getting by.

Finally, we made it to the dump area where the mill stored the log rafts. We started making short runs, picking up lots of sunken logs, and figured we were finally going to make good money. We would get paid when the logs were used by the mill; we got nothing while they were in the cold deck. When we picked up logs by the dam, they were run directly into the mill and we were paid right away; when

---

[13] Boise Cascade purchased the Valsetz sawmill and timber in 1959. This was 1960. When Boise shut down operations in 1984, Valsetz became a ghost town. In 1988 the lake was drained. http://en.wikipedia.org/wiki/Valsetz,_Oregon

we got to the dump area, the mill cold decked the logs to use later and we would get paid later when the logs were used.

Valsetz was an old logging town where workers shopped at the company store. Customers could pay cash or pay in the form of cardboard scrip, whose face value was marked up 10%. The scrip went against what the workers were due at the pay office. Scrip was the store's way of managing purchases made on credit. While we were cold decking logs and not drawing any pay, we used scrip to buy what we needed from the store.

After we got the cold deck built up, the mill manager said, "I don't want you salvaging anymore of those logs."

"What's wrong?" we asked.

"Well, we can't pay you for those logs," he said.

"Why can't you pay us?" After all, this was Boise Cascade, a big corporation.

"Those logs sank before they were scaled (measured) and we pay the loggers on water scale," he explained. He said it was a big problem for them. "If we pay you, we have to pay the loggers, too."

As long as the logs stayed in the cold deck they didn't have to pay anyone.

Here we were. We were broke and they had this big pile of logs we'd salvaged, but they wouldn't pay us for them. We ate a lot of deer.

We got another job in Toledo, near Newport, Oregon. Once again, we moved our equipment in the middle of the night.

Meanwhile, we got hold of an attorney to start proceedings to sue Boise Cascade. We were two little guys; we were crazy to think we were going to sue Boise Cascade.

Chapter 14: End of a Partnership

Richard and I went to the same guy we got the old Medco trailer from and bought two new 40-foot house trailers in different colors.

While Richard and I lived in Newport with our families, our salvage projects in nearby Toledo only kept us busy part time and I got a steady job doing boat repair in a marina.

Another friend of mine was interested in diving and I hired him to help us out. Keith Wilson was a year older than me and a friend from high school. My partner, Richard, was tall—about 6'1"—and athletic; we didn't always agree on how to do things. Keith and I were more similar in temperament and build; we worked well together. (Later, when we worked for Devine's, we always tended each other; we knew what the other was doing—we knew what the other needed without talking about it much.)

Right out of high school, Keith worked at Hasssell Fabrication in Ashland as a machinist and welder making log bunks. Like I did at the same age, he figured, *I'm not going to be doing this the rest of my life.* On a lunch break one day, he was looking through a magazine and saw an ad in the back of a diving magazine that caught his attention and enrolled in the Al Mikalow School of Deep Sea Diving in Oakland, California. (It's interesting that out of a high

Keith Wilson at diving school, Oakland, California (1958)

school class of only 102, two of us became professional divers.) I got Keith started diving with a double tank and a spear gun on Lake of the Woods in southern Oregon, the same lake I had my first dive. We created our own dive club, the Rogue River Divers, by painting the name of the club on a rock. We were the only members.

After dive school, Keith went into the Army where he worked as a supply sergeant; we kept in touch via letters.

After the Army, when Keith came to work with me, he stayed with Sandy, Laurie, and me in our house trailer in Newport, Oregon. Even with the baby crying all the time, the arrangement worked out well. Keith had a BSA motorcycle. I'd never had a motorcycle and couldn't resist taking Keith's across the Newport Bridge—much too fast. At the time, it was great, but afterwards I told myself, *Ken, there are a lot of things you want to do with your life, and, if you keep this up, you're not going to make it.*

Keith and I used to go diving on the jetty for ling cod. One time someone gave us a seven-foot wolf eel he had caught and we filleted it out. I told Keith, "We're going to fool Sandy; we'll tell her it's ling cod." It didn't taste any different.

Another time I shot a big old raccoon. Keith asked me, "What are we going to do with it?"

I smiled and said, "We'll cook it up and tell Sandy it's rabbit."

When work at the log salvage project was slow, I told Richard, "Why don't you and Keith go work the salvage job and I'll keep my job at the marina?"

In order to pay off our company debts—including a new dive compressor I'd purchased from Uncle Blackie's friend, Leonard—I held down three jobs: during the day, I worked at the marina; when a third hand was needed, I worked at log salvage; swing shift I worked from on an offshore drill platform where Keith and I picked up jobs core drilling the Newport, Oregon, harbor entrance.

When the log salvage work in Toledo was finished, Keith and I worked on the offshore drilling job until it was finished the following spring. Richard returned to school to finish the teaching degree he had dropped when we got the Medco job.

A year later Richard and I had our day in court with Boise Cascade; the judge awarded us the full amount of our claim, but Richard and I never worked together again.

Chapter 15: A New Partnership

THE PLATFORM Keith and I worked from was located just off the mouth of the river in Newport, Oregon. We were doing core drilling to determine the type of material to be dredged in order to enlarge the harbor entrance. One night, a big storm flipped the drill platform into the sea outside of the bay. The construction company hired Keith and me to dive and recover the equipment; this was my first crack at non-log salvage. The owner of the construction company, an engineer named Troxell, liked that Keith and I were divers.

In the fall of 1960, Troxell invited Keith and me to go to Pasco for a job on the Snake River. I still had my house trailer and the equipment from the partnership with Richard, which was now dissolved.

The Pasco job involved equipping barges with equipment for drilling holes in the bottom of the Snake River and loading the holes with explosives to shoot and break up the solid-rock river bottom for digging a navigation channel below Ice Harbor Dam, the first dam to be built on the Snake River.[14] Troxell wanted Keith and me to be welders and drillers. He said we could take our pick of the barges and our pick of shifts; we were to build barges, drill holes in the bottom of the river, and blow up bedrock.

I worked swing shift and Keith worked graveyard. Keith remembers it as the coldest job we were ever on—the icicles were two feet long and stuck out horizontally from the wind. Even when we weren't diving we wore wet suits to stay warm.

Each barge had a track and a core drill. Using a sextant to mark our position, we drilled a hole in the river bottom, inserted an aluminum tube, and loaded it with dynamite and primer cord. The drill moved down the track. When we had thirteen holes drilled and primed, we stood off with the barge, and blew the primed holes;

---

[14] "Ten miles above its confluence with the Columbia River, the first dam to be built on the Snake (River) in the early 1960s was Ice Harbor, a 130-million-dollar structure of concrete and steel. In addition to its power-generating and fish-passage facilities, a navigation lock of 675 feet long and 100 feet high was installed to handle barge traffic." – Page 276, *The Dam Builders* by Bill Gulick, 1971

then we did it again. We drilled and blew sixty-some holes a night. The next day, other guys came out with a digging bucket and a barge and took out the loose rock.

It was fun and we made good money.

Sandy, Laurie and I were living in the trailer when Carrie was born in Pasco on March 17, 1962. Our lives were in turmoil with projects here and there, but Sandy and I wanted another baby. Sandy had little trouble with delivery this time. Laurie was almost five; we were concerned she would miss her place as the center of attention, but when we brought Carrie home, Laurie took on the role of little mother.

The Pasco job went through the winter. The work was hard and cold and we decided we needed to do something different. As spring rolled around and the job was coming to an end, I asked Keith if he wanted to go into partnership with me and back into the log salvage business.

On August 5, 1963, Keith and I drew up an agreement.

First, we needed to determine where to find logs to salvage. We drove down from Pasco, Washington, to Portland, Oregon, for a couple of dives on the Willamette River. Log rafts lined the shore. We could walk out on the rafts and jump in at any point and find sunken logs.

We needed a buyer for our logs and contacted Publishers Paper, a mill in Oregon City using hemlock logs to make paper. They showed an interest in buying the logs we salvaged. Publishers wanted the logs delivered on a truck to the mill with the old, water-soaked ends cut off so they could see the grain.

The middle of the river was under the control of the State, which sold permission to pick up free-floating logs, deadheads and sunken logs. The State took a fee for each log salvaged in the middle of the river; we didn't have to pay the State a fee for the logs we found under company-owned log rafts.

We contacted Crown Zellerbach, which had extensive log-storage areas along the edges of the river, for permission to salvage their sunken logs, too.

Mr. Mellors, the head of Crown Zellerbach Logging, was in his sixties and close to retirement. When I called, he agreed to see us. Keith and I went up to see him in his office in one of the tall buildings in downtown Portland. We told him, "We are in the log salvage business. We are going to be moving in on the river and salvaging logs under an Oregon State Log Patrol license arrangement and we are interested in salvaging the logs underneath your storage grounds."

Our license with the State let us salvage logs in the channel, but did not allow us to go under log rafts or into the log rafting area. Mr. Mellors had never heard of us. I had just turned 23 and Keith was 24.

"Do you boys have a piece of property that you are going to be operating off of to load the logs and cut the ends?" he asked us.

"Not yet. We want to locate above the falls and work the upper part of the river."

"Well, we've got a couple of acres at the upper end of the liquor pond (used for settling out chemicals used by the mill to make paper). Do you want to use that?"

"Yes," we said.

"There are some people you need to know," he told us. They all worked for Crown Z. One was in charge of logging operations in Oregon City. Another was in charge of log movement on the river. There was a third guy, but I don't remember specifically what role he had.

"I'll make the calls and tell them about you," Mr. Mellors promised.

Here he had given us a job, property to work off of, and contacts, yet he had never seen us before.

The meeting was very reminiscent of my meeting two years ago with Medco, and before that with the manager at Croft & Neville. Something happened to give these men confidence in us. I believe these men were guided to use us—when I left their offices, each one of them probably scratched his head and wondered why he agreed to work with me. I did not hear the voice tell me I was going to work for Medco, Publishers or Crown Zellerbach like I did with Croft & Neville, but the results were the same.

The old pontoon barge Keith and I had from my previous partnership with Richard wasn't big enough or powerful enough to do what we needed on the Willamette. We had to start again and build new equipment.

When the dam job in Pasco was finished, Keith and I moved our operations down to the Portland area. It was May and Sandy had just had Carrie a couple months earlier. This time we rented a house in Gladstone.

Keith and I somehow needed to get the equipment together for our new venture. It was a different operation working on the river versus lakes; we had to travel further on the water and had strong currents to deal with. We also needed to deliver the logs to Publishers by land, not water. We had to set up a river operation and a land operation all at once.

The problem was, we were broke. I mean, we didn't have any money. I had let my car go back to the bank because I couldn't make payments; I had a little equity in it so they took it without hurting my credit. I gave the house trailer to someone in return for taking over payments,

Keith and I needed to build a larger barge with inboard motors; we got busy and started negotiating for steel.

As kids in high school, Keith and I had done a lot of car work. Keith still had an old Plymouth in a shop at his folks' house in Ashland. We drove down and towed it to Gladstone where Sandy and I were renting a house.

To build the barge and engines, we needed first to build a welder. We went down to Zidell Marine where they were scrapping out old ships and made friends with one of the guys that ran it. We told him our story and he wanted to help. We told him we needed a generator that we could use to make a welder. There were big electric welders from the ships just sitting out in the dirt. He sold us the generator end of an electric welder and we coupled it to the Plymouth engine to convert it into a gas-powered welder. We mounted the engine and generator end to the Plymouth's front axle, added a gravity-fed gas tank mounted above the engine, and, *voila*, we had a gas-powered generator we could tow to job sites. It was hokey, but it worked.

We already had an old flatbed with an A-frame on it that we used to set the heavy equipment.

We bought some steel on credit and started putting the pontoons together, but we still needed engines. At the time, a lot of small pleasure boats had a flathead six cylinder engine called a Chrysler Crown that was being replaced with a newer, faster V8. The Chrysler Crowns were good engines and transmissions, and there were a lot of them around, but we couldn't afford them. That didn't stop us.

Keith and I drove to marinas and repair yards all over the countryside. We got scrap parts from junk heaps, most of them for nothing. We found a couple of old blocks, cranks, engine parts, and transmissions. We brought it all back to the house I'd rented, spread the parts on the floor of the one-car garage, and started building engines. We needed two of each part. Re-bore the blocks, re-machine the cranks, add new bearings, pistons, gaskets, etc., and we were building engines.

Late one night, when everyone else was in bed, Keith and I were putting our first engine together. It was set on timbers. "Heck," we figured, "this thing is ready to run." We put in a little gas and fired it up. It ran great. But it didn't have any mufflers and we woke up the whole neighborhood.

Keith and I took the two Chrysler Crown engines we'd rebuilt down to the property Crown Z lent to us. We built the pontoons on site. From the rear end of the old Plymouth we made a right-angled drive with a reduction and took an engine out of an Austin Healy automobile to make a power winch; now we wouldn't have to crank the logs up by hand like we did on the Medco project.

The barge was designed to haul a couple of logs between the pontoons and, using the outriggers, we could haul a bunch of logs alongside the barge. We averaged 10,000 board feet of logs per load with one load per day. We were getting $35 per thousand board feet from Publishers, less $5 to the brand owner, such as Crown Z, leaving us about $300 a day.

Once we had enough logs on the beach to make a load, we had to figure out how to get the logs out of the river and onto the truck. In the beginning, we made arrangements with the fellow at a leasing company for logging equipment. We leased a heel boom for so much per thousand board feet on the scale—that way he got paid when we got paid. We used some logs to make a cribbing, backfilled it with dirt so we could get the heel boom out over the river to pick up logs, swing them around, and load them onto the truck. We hired a truck driver and away he went with our logs to the mill.

We were in business. However, by the time we paid the truck driver and the lease on the heel boom, we weren't making enough to be worth it so we decided to get our own equipment.

We had a log deck, but no money and we were starving. We decided to try to get our first loan. We went to First National, the bank where we'd had accounts for years, to see the loan officer—he wouldn't talk to us. "How do we know the logs are worth anything?" he asked us. We got up, went across the street to US Bank, and talked to Bruce Colson. He was intrigued with our operation and gave us a loan.

Like Bruce, other people went out of their way to help us. Al Haberlack, the wholesale distributor for Standard Oil Fuel Products, had a bulk fuel station next to the Grange co-op in Gladstone; he was wonderful. Al was so intrigued with our operation that he got us a deal where we could buy our fuel through Standard Oil; it was a useful line of credit. We met his son, Larry, who was 14 at the time. He and Keith are still friends.

We bought an old logging donkey that was setting out in the woods and went to a used truck company that had an old logging truck sitting out back in the weeds. We made a deal with the guy—if we could use his shop and his yard to rebuild the truck, we'd buy it from him; on credit, of course.

We rebuilt the truck engine, painted the body orange, the steelwork black, and the wheels silver. It was very attractive.

After we got the truck all fixed up, we went into the woods to get the logging donkey. The winch was powered with a Ford 60, which was the first V8 Ford Motor Company came out with. We hauled the donkey to the site, rigged up a haul back from the logging donkey to the river, and built an A-frame out of logs; we'd hook up the logs, pull them up with the donkey, and cold deck them. We used the haul back to stack the logs against a big old cottonwood tree; the stack of logs sloped out from the tree. When we had a large cold deck of logs built, we backed our truck under the A-frame, loaded the truck with logs, and hauled them to the mill. The process wasn't much different from what I had learned at the logging camp when I was a kid.

We'd load the logs onboard the truck and head over to the other side of the river, using Willamette Falls Drive out of the town of Willamette, to Publishers to dump the logs. Later, when we had trouble with the mill manager at Publishers, we went to mills as far as Newberg, about twenty miles each way, with our loads. We normally hauled on Wednesday, Thursday and Friday. Saturday through Tuesday we were on the river salvaging logs and building a new cold deck. We did that for about five or six years, and, since it only took the two of us to do the work, we were making money. The mill paid us at the end of each week. We used that money to pay off our accumulated company debt, which was considerable.

During our work salvaging logs someone called Keith and me "Lucky Dogs." He had no idea of the amount of work that went into our "luck!"

As far as we know, we were the only people that ever had a contract with Crown Zellerbach to salvage sunken logs. The sunken logs had been building up forever; some peeler logs were seven feet across and one brand we found was from before WWI. We salvaged 20 miles of river from the Yamhill River on the west side to Willamette Falls; we did some salvage below the falls, too. The work was great;

it was dark working in the river, but we didn't think anything of it. We worked 24/7, including Thanksgiving.

By March 1964, about six months after starting operations on the river, we were out of debt; every week the money we made went into paying off our debts. The last week in February we took that week's paycheck, shut down operations, and went on vacation to southern California—with our diving gear, of course.

By this time my daughter Laurie was almost seven, Carrie was almost two, and Sandy was pregnant with our son, Eric. I left the kids and Sandy with my parents in Newport Beach while Keith and his girlfriend and I went to Mexico for a few days to dive in warm, clear water. We camped on the beach, dove, and ate lobster.

After a month of vacation, we all came back to where we had left off, but without the debt hanging over us like a huge weight. Now we could focus on making money to invest. That's when Keith and I started building apartments. Plus we were still salvaging logs. Keith ran the donkey and I hooked the logs and loaded them onto the truck. I'd give Keith the signal to release the logs onto the truck and I'd drive off to the mill. While I was gone with the load, Keith and his brother would cut log ends and add our brand, KK, for Ken and Keith.

The mill manager was a bit of a jerk. Our agreement with Publishers Paper was with the log buyer, who told us what percent of rot could be on the ends, acceptable log sizes, etc. I don't know why the mill manager had it in for us. It all came to a head one rainy day after we had been working there for a while. I had my rain gear on and was tired and exhausted from working. By this time the truck was pretty beat up, too. I drove under the crane where the mill unloaded our logs. Here came the Publishers mill manager, who had nothing to do with buying logs. He had a new Polaroid camera and was taking pictures of the ends of our logs. I knew he was up to no good. He was trying to get us run off. There had been words before that gave me the impression he didn't like me much, but I didn't know why.

You SOB, I said to myself, *I'll get a piece of your ass.*

I took off my rain gear. "What's the problem?" I asked him. I was trying to stay cool.

"Get this load out of here. I'm not accepting this load. Get it out of here," he ordered.

"You've got nothing to do with it." I was firm. "The truck's not moving until the logs are unloaded and there's no man here that can make me move it!"

He choked up and blustered, "I'll get the log buyer, then."

"That's your only choice," I said.

The log buyer came out, looked at the load, and told the mill manager, "Unload 'em."

You get pushed to a point where you can't handle it. There are people out there who want to destroy you; you may or may not know why. The important thing is to know where you stand and hold your ground without making the situation worse and not hold a grudge when it's over; you have to be willing to shake hands afterwards.

As I said before, I ran illegal loads, but not always. I ran a legal load. Once.... When we took salvaged logs to the mill, they were waterlogged. It looked like a legal load because you couldn't see the waterlogged logs were so heavy. The mills didn't care how much the logs weighed. The last load of the day one Friday, the day we tried to get our landing cleared out so we could dive for more logs, I gave Keith the signal to shut down.

"Why?" he asked. "You have room for another log and there's one more log laying there."

I think it was the only time Keith and I disagreed.

"I think this is a legal load," I told him. "I've got a bad feeling."

Keith wasn't too happy. As I pulled out onto the highway, I came upon the highway patrol with a portable jump scale. The trailer was two hundred pounds light and the tractor was four hundred pounds heavy. The officer said, "That's not enough to worry about. We won't give you a ticket."

As I climbed back into the truck, the officer added, "Cover your ass. You've got an enemy."

It had to be the mill manager. After that, Keith and I went right back to hauling as much as we could carry. It was the only legal load we ever hauled and the only one where we were challenged. Someone or something was watching out for me.

There was a platform on a landing at the mill where the mill manager could watch the unloading process. For a long time after our disagreement, I didn't see him. Then one day I was bringing in a load and he came out and waved. A few years later, after he retired from Publishers and I had purchased my first marina, he came down to our floating restaurant at Sportcraft Landing and we had a good laugh over the whole thing.

One day, Keith and I were putting a new engine in the old orange logging truck when a storm hit. The wind came up in the late afternoon. There were cottonwood trees all around the little shack where we were working. We ran down to the river to tie up our logging barge to secure it against the high wind. When we came back to the shack, trees were falling. The shack didn't provide any protection, so we went under the truck. A tree fell across the truck, but did not damage it seriously enough that we couldn't drive it.

Of course, our standards for what was safe to drive may have been different than other people's. For example, one day Keith heard someone say "Look! Somebody's getting ready to jump out of that truck!" I wasn't getting ready to jump—the door latch didn't work and I was holding the door closed with one hand and shifting with the other hand.

When we pulled loads out of the operation at the river we had to climb all the way up the hill—this was using the old road before I-205 went in—and we had to have the truck in low gear. The old Chevy engine was worn out and we had replaced it with a Chrysler V8—we needed the extra power for our overly large loads.

Keith got this wild idea to put double stacks on the truck. We took the drivelines out of two old trucks and used them for muffler stacks—they were incredibly loud. I'm sure all the neighbors hated us. Once, in the middle of the day, I was coming down the steep incline by the West Linn Bridge. The bridge was at a slant. I was on compression and I needed to brake it—the megaphone muffler stacks on the truck were so loud I could see the glass in the store windows in Oregon City vibrate. I told Keith we needed to tune them down. We put in baffles and it was better.

Chapter 16: Fire in the Hole

A COUPLE of years after launching the new barge, we needed to haul it for repairs. We dry docked it at Sportcraft Landing, the marina I would later own. Keith sent his brother, also named Norman, like my brother, into one of the pontoons to drain the gas from a leaking fuel tank so we could repair it. Keith and I went to the aft end to work underneath the pontoon on the rudder and shaft.

Norman used two five-gallon steel containers to transfer the fuel from the leaking fifty-gallon tank to the tank in the other pontoon. He ran the gas spigot to fill one can while he carried a full can to the other tank. While sitting around waiting for a can to fill, he cushioned himself from the steel frames using a mat from the old Plymouth. Each pontoon was a twenty to thirty-foot-long rectangular tube about three-feet deep and three-and-a-half-feet wide. An engine was mounted in the middle of each pontoon about a third of the way up from the aft end with a hatch above the engine. The fuel tanks were mounted above and a little forward of each engine. To get to the hatch and put the full can on deck, Norman had bend over and squeeze past the engine, dragging the heavy can on the other side of the engine.

It was hard work. Norman decided to change the routine a bit and ended up dragging the metal can of gasoline across the batteries.

The spark melted a hole in the can.

The hole in the can drained flaming gas into the bilge.

As he tried to escape, Norman tripped over the second gas can and tipped it into the bilge.

To make it worse, the spigot on fuel tank was open and draining gasoline directly into the bilge, feeding the fire. Norman was caught in a steel chamber of hot fumes. Flames were shooting through the hatch. He crawled as best he could into the bow, dragging the car mat with him, and putting it over his face.

Keith and I heard the *whoomp* of gas igniting and Norman's screams. We saw black smoke streaming out of the hatch. Keith took one of the dive bottles and regulators and tossed it into the barge for Norman to use for air. We needed to cut off air to the fire, so I slammed the hatch closed to kill the flames. This also killed off the air to Norman. I didn't know what else to do. However, Keith had the presence of mind to jump off the barge and turn off the acetylene to the cutting torch, leaving the oxygen turned on.

Keith yelled to me, "I got to get this oxygen to Norman!"

When I lifted the hatch, hot gas fumes were going to pour out. If there was even one spark when I opened the hatch, the hot gases were going to blow. Keith lay down on the deck. It was hot. I opened the hatch. Keith threw the torch as hard as he could toward Norman, screaming, "Pick up the torch! Pick up the torch! Put it in your mouth!"

Pretty soon, Norman put together the pieces of what we were yelling and put the torch end in his mouth. The oxygen saved his lungs and his life. The open hatch let the hot fumes pour out and the cold air go in. We kept yelling at Norman and he eventually crawled out of the open hatch with only superficial burns.

There was never a spark, it didn't blow! The only damages to the pontoon were some burned wires on the motor. Norman went to the hospital to get his burns treated. He was back to work in a week or so. It was a miracle he wasn't killed or more seriously burned.

I don't know how, under this extreme condition, Keith had the presence of mind to do what he did to save Norm's life. Was he spiritually guided? I think so. I've always thought there was something special about Keith. On the surface, he was an average student who loved hot rods, but I've never known anyone who didn't like him—they can sense there is something special about him.

We finished the repairs to the barge and re-launched it. Once we got several miles of logs cleared out, we needed more range and bought a 42' river tug with twin Cummings diesels.

The Willamette River project lasted about three years. Each day we took three truckloads of logs out of the river—a load was a banded group of logs of 7,500 board feet and we could carry three loads at a time on the barge for 22,500 board feet a day. In all, we figure we salvaged two million board feet from the bottom of the river.

During that time, I bought a one-year-old, three bedroom house in Gladstone. Our son Eric was born May 30, 1964, when Carrie was two and Laurie was seven.

Chapter 17: The *Mackmarie*

WHILE DOING log salvage, Keith and I also successfully salvaged, rebuilt and sold a few small boats we found, including an old 26' Chris Craft cabin cruiser we found at a moorage and a sunken ski boat from the Columbia. Keith and I were diving for logs by Wilsonville when we found a sunk wood trawler. We contacted an insurance company to see if we could get salvage rights. We had a crane from Bernert Towing lift the wreck. We used a P500 military pump we got from Zidell Marine (a company that scrapped old military vessels, mostly Liberty ships, and used the steel to build barges) to pump out the water and mud; then we towed the boat through the locks at the dam in Oregon City and tied up at Sportcraft Landing. Ruth Huff, one of the owners of Sportcraft at the time, had a good view of the wreck and determined it was the *Mackmarie*. (I later purchased Sportcraft Landing from the Huffs). Keith and I were going to fix her up, and we did get some old anchors and other hardware off of the wreck, but the boat was too far gone to repair. Keith was in love and didn't spend as much time on the project as I did. While he and Linda were away on their honeymoon, I had a crane move the *Mackmarie* up to a gravel bar, poured some diesel on it, and burned it. Barry Huff and his mother, Ruth, wrote a poem about it.

The Mackmarie, Willamette River (1960)

The Foul Raising of the *Mackmarie*

A faint light funneled through the murky sea

Where lay the ghostly hull of the *Mackmarie*.

Silent currents lapped its rotting beams.

Soft slime oozed in gaping seams.

Yet strangely peaceful was this grave,

Caressed and blessed by deep deep waves.

Now what strange power did this corpse possess

That would cause me to descend these dreamy depths

And from the bowels of the undulating sea

Raise the grotesque hull of the *Mackmarie*?

Why is tortured timber and crumbling deck

And mouldering bow of this slumbering wreck

Exposed in all its ghastly blight

To living flesh and merciless light?

Who were the ghouls that robbed this watery grave?

Oh, just Dye and Wilson, the dirty knaves!

Chapter 18: Story of the first *Que Sera*

If salvaging the old, wooden *Mackmarie* from the bottom of the Willamette River may not have gone as planned, I had much better luck bringing a steel sailboat back to life. It was winter, 1973, when I read an article about the grounding of the *Que Sera Sera* off the Oregon Coast near Waldport.

My dive partner at the time, Kent Cochrane, and I went to the motel where the owners of the wreck were staying and asked if they wanted us to salvage the *Que Sera Sera* for them, but Joe Browning and his wife had had enough of cruising and offered to sell what was left of her to us for $1,000.

On that first day, we went down to the beach to see the wreck. Even though she was buried in the beach, and her hull was full of sand, I was amazed and thought, *This is a miracle. That boat is a very, very strong boat; even though it was mashed, it didn't break.* Some of the seams had cracked and let water in. The house was gone and water had also come in through the broken windows. I went back to the motel to buy the boat and learn her history. The Brownings told me about two jewelry cases containing Mrs. Browning's gems that they hoped to recover. (Later, when one of my guys found the gems, he got all excited until I told him, "No, no, we've got to give that back.")

The sleek 60-foot steel sailboat was built in The Netherlands in 1955 by the owner of a barge company as a wedding gift for his daughter. From The Netherlands she sailed to Australia where she was sold to a new owner who named her *Sundowner*. Eventually, she found her way to the West Coast of the United States, where she was anchored in San Diego harbor for a number of years while receiving little care.

It was in San Diego that recently-retired Joe Browning and his wife found the vessel and named her *Que Sera Sera*. They sold their San Diego Taco Bell franchise, one of the first, to their kids and used the proceeds to buy their first boat and a bagful of $25.00 gold sovereigns. In the fall of 1973, the Brownings began to motor up the West Coast to Puget Sound where they planned to upgrade the boat. As the couple motored north, they visited friends—it was late November before they reached the Oregon Coast.

Just outside of Waldport, Oregon, they were hit by a tremendous storm. Joe was not yet an accomplished sailor and his wife had a heart condition; she was below and couldn't help Joe at the helm. Alone, Joe couldn't head the boat out to sea, so he radioed in to enter several small harbors, but each time was turned away by the Coast Guard, telling him the bar was too dangerous to navigate. They should have told him all the ports were closed and to head out to sea. Instead, Joe hugged the coast looking for an open port.

Old Joe was outside in the weather getting cold and tired. The boat didn't have inside steering then—I added that later. At the time, the cockpit had an eight-inch frame with two drains plumbed in such a way they went inside, through the engine room, and then outside. Unbeknownst to Joe, the drain elbows had rusted through. As the sea water from the large waves and swells washed over the deck and filled the cockpit, part of the seawater flowing through the drains went overboard, and part of the water went into the bilges. When the water level got to the engine, it killed it.

The November wind and waves drenched Joe. He realized he was getting into hypothermia and needed to do something. His wife was still down below and it was too stormy to sail single handed.

With the engine dead and too tired to sail singlehanded, Joe dropped the anchor about a quarter mile off shore. It was a good anchor with all chain rode so it should hold. Unbeknownst to Joe, the bitter end of the anchor rode wasn't attached to the hull—he helplessly watched the chain feed out the end of the anchor roller and go to the bottom of the sea.

As the storm pushed the *Que Sera Sera* toward the beach, Joe went below and told his wife, "We're going to go aground."

He tied her into her bunk then did the same thing to himself.

The huge surf rolled the boat over and over in the sea and it hit the sand—hard. The impacts tore off the rigging, crushed the house, and smashed the hull, but the hull stayed together (the seams were butt welded and riveted to a backing plate). When the boat quit bouncing into the beach, Joe and his wife waded ashore.

The Brownings told the Coast Guard about the bag of gold; the Coast Guard went out and sawed a hole in the hull and got it out for them.

Soon after the purchase, Kent and I returned to the *Que Sera Sera* at low tide. That was when I realized the hull was full of sixty-five tons of sand—sand that would have to come out before the boat could be pulled from the hole in the beach. I set up a salvage operation with several hands made up of friends of mine and kids who worked at Sportcraft, the first marina I owned. I needed people who could shovel and pump sand faster than the next high tide could come in, which filled the hull with sand again. We used two large Cats—one equipped with a large logging drum (a large winch), and the other with a backhoe for digging. My strategy was to work during low tide to remove the sand from around the hull to create a depression around the hull that would fill with water, use water to pump out the sand, dry the hull as best we could, and then break the suction between the sand and the hull so the vessel could be pulled from the beach.

Que Sera Sera in the sand at Waldport, Oregon (Jan. 1974)

The sand continued to challenge us; we never did get the buoyancy factor to work for us. The problem was that the crew pumped sand out all day while the tide was going out, and the incoming tide brought it back, refilling the hull with sand. After seven days and an investment of more than $8,000, I told my crew, "We'll make one more attempt; if we can't get it this time, we're gonna ditch the whole project."

This time the Cats pulled hard enough to cause the hull to vibrate. The vibration did the job—it caused the sand and water to mix in solution, creating a thin semi-liquid space between the hull and the hard sand. The liquid sand supported the hull. The vessel rose two feet up, but she did not move forward. During the few seconds the boat was raised, sand filled in under the boat keeping the boat high.

The next day we came back and continued our work. We had to pump out the sand that had come back in with the tide, but now that the deck was two feet higher, the incoming tide didn't sink the boat as fast as it had before, so there was less sand in the hull. With only about half as much sand in the hull as on previous efforts, the Cats went back to work.

Que Sera Sera being pulled loose from the sand (1974)

Little by little, *Que Sera Sera* let go of the sand. The Cats pulled her up onto the beach, over the sand dunes, and onto a little dirt road just outside of Waldport where we loaded the boat onto a trailer and hauled her to Sportcraft Landing, which I now owned.

We set her up in cribbing on the shore of the Willamette River under the protection of the newly-constructed I-205 bridge in Oregon City. I didn't ask permission, I just did it. Any official going by just assumed I had permission and I never got a hard time about it.

After we got the boat back to Oregon City, it became obvious this was a total rebuild job, not a salvage job. Kent lost interest in the project and I bought him out.

She sat under the bridge for about four years before I could get to it. The year after salvaging her from the beach, I was busy running Sportcraft, salvaging a barge in Alaska and a dredge in Mexico, getting a divorce from Sandy, and meeting my future wife, Kathy, and her two sons. It was a busy year!

After Kathy and I married and settled in at the float home at Sportcraft, we got back to rebuilding the sailboat. At one point during the project, Kathy was in the engine room bucketing out sand and found a billfold stuffed thick with money. We dried it out and saved it for Joe. The Brownings had moved to Brookings, Oregon. I called and told them we were coming down for a visit. They were very pleased to see us. We told them about our progress rebuilding the boat. I pulled the billfold out of my pocket and said, "Joe, we found something that belongs to you."

Joe was surprised and delighted. He went over to this wife and whispered something in her ear. She nodded. He went into the other room and came back out with a gold sovereign and gave it to Kathy. She made it into a necklace. She loves it, but says she is too scared to wear it because she doesn't want to lose it.

It took ten years to rebuild the sailboat. The first order of business was to remove the bent hull plates and ribbing on the port side. *Que Sera Sera*'s hull was crushed inwards for thirty feet amidships. I couldn't get patterns for the frames without recreating the original shape. I cut out one side of the wrinkled steel and built ribs of wood, with strakes fore and aft. Every third wood frame was adjustable. I fine-tuned the adjustable frames until the strake boards fared to the bow and the stern. That gave me a picture of what the original hull looked like.

After I was done, I hated it. I hated the hull. I walked around it for three days and thought about it. I asked myself, *What can I do with this mess? I cannot build it back the way it was.* Apparently the barge company owner didn't know how to build a sailboat. He used a cruising keel, but it looked like he attached it to an hourglass racing hull. The combination of a racing hull on a cruising keel was not a good one. Using the adjustable frames I recreated the hull shape with a belly in it. Once I was happy that the hull and keel were compatible, I fashioned heavy steel ribs in pairs and attached them to the deck and keel on fourteen-inch centers. We drew steel plates over the ribs, creating a soft chine hull.

My brother-in-law, Bill, worked for Gunderson Brothers as a welder. Gunderson makes commercial barges and train cars. Bill volunteered to help weld up the new steel plate. All seams were first welded on the inside with 6011 rod.

Outside I scarfed the seams to create a perfectly clean channel and Bill finished with filler weld.

When both sides were completed, I asked Bill, "How do you feel about the quality of your welds?"

Without hesitation he told me, "Ken, I'll guarantee it one hundred percent." The only question he had was one small spot behind one of the frames where he couldn't see the weld puddle. That was almost 40 years ago and there hasn't been a problem.

Because of the changes to the hull shape, the boat now had two giant indents fore and aft. I went ahead and built it that way and afterwards used filler to fill in the indents. I made a cruising hull out of a racing hull.

I replaced the original concrete ballast with lead, carefully measured and placed to balance the hull to ensure the boat would remain stable. I added a wheelhouse to protect the helmsman from the Pacific Northwest weather. It's constructed of aluminum to keep the weight low topsides. The corners of the pilothouse are rounded and the windows glazed with half-inch safety glass. The deck rails are welded stainless steel tubes.

A ship's architect drew up a sail plan based on the original design of the vessel. He confirmed that the configuration was balanced with the new hull shape. I replaced the original wood spars and mast with new aluminum ones made in Canada. Every component of the rigging is heavier than that found on manufactured boats. For example, the stays are 3/8-inch stainless steel cable and the sockets are poured with lead and affixed to heavy-duty turn buckles fixed to heavy stainless steel pad eyes.

The boat is fitted with a built-in twelve-cubic-foot freezer located under a bunk. Heavy, rigid, blow-in foam insulation isolates the freezer, fuel and water tanks from the hull. Two cold plates running off an isolated pump provide refrigeration. To test its performance, I brought the freezer temperature to below zero and turned off the pump. It took seven days to raise the temperature to thirty-two degrees. I figure a half-filled freezer will stay below freezing for at least two weeks if the refrigeration unit fails.

Below decks, the boat sleeps six with a master bunk forward and a stateroom with a double bunk aft of that. The main cabin has a built-in settee and the café-style table drops to make up into another double bunk. To keep the boat warm in cool, damp Pacific Northwest weather, I put in two stoves—a diesel heater fitted to the amidships bulkhead and a miniature version of the enameled iron trash burner stove we had in the house when I was a kid.

There are two heads, one with a shower. All cabinetry is custom built and the galley is first class. The interior is finished with fiddle back black walnut harvested from a tree I salvaged. I watched that tree for years. It was huge and leaned out over the Willamette River. I knew it would come down one day in a big wind. When it finally happened, I picked it up and had it rough cut into lumber, which I stacked and dried.

At last in 1983, her name shortened to *Que Sera*, the vessel was rigged and ready for her shakedown cruise. My second wife Kathy and I cruised to British Columbia to go sightseeing and diving. On the return trip, we stayed one night in Grays Harbor, Washington. While Kathy was still sleeping, I set out for Portland without checking the tides or sea conditions. Once underway and cruising at about eight knots, I looked out at the Grays Harbor bar. All I could see was white.

It was a dangerous situation; the swells were coming in and the tide was going out, causing the swells to increase in height until the Coast Guard closed the bar. That didn't stop me. I said to myself, *Well, what the hell. It's a shakedown cruise. Let's go for it.* The swells reached forty feet and there was often fifteen feet or more of green water higher than the transom. As I headed toward the bottom of a particularly steep trough, I was sure I was going to dive the bow into the trough, but as the bow hit the bottom of the trough, it went in but not under; at the same time, I spun my head around and saw the canoe-stern transom chop the swell we were on in half—the bow forced the smaller-displacement stern to cut into the swell. In spite of the four-story-high swells, I didn't get any green water over the deck.

As we cleared the last swell, I felt my boat smile. The conditions had challenged her and she enjoyed the victory as much as I did.

As *Que Sera* reached the Columbia River and safe water, Kathy came stumbling out of the house and asked, "What happened?" She had been sleeping in the forward bunk when we left port; as *Que Sera* and I climbed the swells and dropped into the troughs she was alternately bounced between the low ceiling and the foam mattress.

"Oh, we just had a little swell," I told her.

Since that day, *Que Sera* has taken me and the family and our friends to Alaska several times. We've explored the West Coast of the United States and Canada diving and fishing, and searching for gold and treasure.

Chapter 19: Who Will Believe Me?

One day, when I was around 25 years old, still married to Sandy and salvaging logs with Keith, I was running the tug up the river and got to thinking. Several things had already happened—all the messages were coming together. The voice had told me things, and it was coming together.

I'd been told I'd be a professional diver and here I was, running a successful business diving for sunken logs and had hopes for doing heavy marine salvage work.

I'd been told Sandy was pregnant and we were able to get married before it became obvious; even her mother never knew.

I'd been told I would work for Croft & Neville and I got the job without any effort. I was hired by Medco, Publisher's Paper Co., and Crown Zellerbach in much the same way.

Now I'm thinking, *Everything that happened to me is so unbelievable. If I try to tell someone about the spiritual messages, they won't believe me.*

I was a pretty straight kid. My parents taught me well, but I was in a marriage that wasn't perfect and I wasn't always honest. I thought, *If I never again tell a lie, then if I tell someone my story, they will have to believe me.*

It took about a year before I felt comfortable enough to test the waters with people I knew well. If it went well, I'd go into more detail. Some people could handle the idea of a spiritual presence that is around us all the time better than others. After experiencing it all my life, I had to accept it

I'd always done what the voice said and it turned out well. Sixteen years later, the voice spoke to me again; this time it was a warning, but I didn't act fast enough and there was a disaster.

Later on in my diving career, I'd know things I had no prior knowledge of; I'd know how to do something or solve a problem that I'd never solved before. In ten years of chasing heavy marine salvage jobs that never failed, there had to be something outside of me guiding me, giving me these clear insights. I couldn't have known and done all I did without it.

By telling these stories from my life, I hope to convince others that there's help—that by being receptive to a spiritual presence, they can receive help, too.

Part 4: Marine Salvage & Sportcraft Landing

Sportcraft Landing as it looked when Ken bought it (circa 1969)

Chapter 20: Meeting Fred Devine

I WENT TO WORK at Fred Devine Diving and Salvage Company in 1965 when I was 26 years old. I met Fred Devine four years earlier on his last dive.[15] One night while I was working at the marina in Newport, Oregon, a wooden research vessel hit the jetty. I dove and put a patch on the hull using a section of plywood and a piece of foam mat from the dining table. I heard Fred Devine was coming to tow the boat back to Portland.

I knew of Devine's for years. They owned the 200-foot, 490-ton *Salvage Chief*, a retired LSM (Landing Ship Medium) that the U.S. Navy used to land tanks and men on beaches during invasions. The *Salvage Chief* was outfitted with three 100-ton winches forward and three 100-ton winches facing aft for tow lines. The vessel was well stocked with pumps and various other pieces of salvage equipment. [16]

Fred Devine, Photo by Larry Barber (date unknown)

I took time off from my marina job in Newport and went down to the site and introduced myself to Fred as he was getting out of the water. He was in his hard helmet dive gear. I told him I was the diver that put on the patch.

"That was a good patch," he said. "If you find yourself in Portland, come on by. I can use scuba divers who know how to work."

After Sandy and I moved to Gladstone, and as Keith and I cleaned out the Willamette River and were running out of logs, I made it a habit to stop by Fred

---

[15] Fred Devine Diving & Salvage Company has been in diving and construction since 1913.
http://freddevinedivingandsalvage.com/

[16] SALVAGE CHIEF IMO No: 5308251, Fred Devine Diving and Salvage Co., Portland OR. Flag: U.S.A. (Portland OR). Comments: May 10, 2007. This ship was built as a Landing Ship Medium, the LSM 380, and saw service in the Pacific during WWII. She was converted to a salvage ship by Fred Devine who purchased her from the Navy. Year built / Builder: 1945, Brown Shipbuilding Co., U.S.A. Details: 787. Dimensions: LOA: 61.75 m b: 10.36 m draught: - m. Main engines: 2, 10 cyl Fairbanks Morse diesel engines Power: 2,650 kW. Max. speed: - knots.
http://ship-pics.co.uk/pancan.htm

Devine's Portland offices to stay in touch. I let him know we were diving every day and ready to go instantly. Every once in a while he needed a scuba diver. Pretty soon, he needed Keith and me more and more.

On the road we'd share a motel room with two beds. Keith spent more time with Morris Devine, Fred's brother. I partnered up with Louie Smith, another of the old-time hard hat divers. Keith didn't get much sleep—Morris smoked a lot and hacked all night. The Devine brothers came from an era where they partied hearty and were hard on themselves.

Ultimately, Keith took over Morris's position and I took over for Louie. We became the main divers and we introduced scuba to Devine.

After working with Devine's for a while, I could see the company was in financial trouble. One day I called Fred Devine at home. The company office was in his son-in-law, Mick Leitz's, basement.

"I want to come to see you, Fred."

"Sure, come on over," he said gruffly. He always had a cigarette hanging out of his mouth and you could hear it in his voice.

When I arrived, I told him, "The competition is picking you apart. You could have these jobs. I can get these jobs for you."

"What do you mean?" he asked.

"I know people in the marine construction business. I just need your permission to contact them."

Fred got excited. He came over and gave me a hug. I started hitting all the big marine construction companies and pretty soon we had work. Doing that was fine, but I wanted to be a professional diver, not a salesman.

Chapter 21: Hypothermia

EARLY IN MY time with Devine's we got a small dive job cutting a large hole in a sheet piling near St. Helens on the Columbia River. It was December, but I was still using my summer wet suit, which worked fine when I was working hard at log salvage. I went to the job with Louie. Louie took the first shift, while I tended. After lunch I put on my summer wet suit, forgetting I'd be using little energy on this job. When you're burning steel, it is important to not move—just pull the burning device slowly along the steel surface. When you come to a joint, it burns even more slowly, and no bodily energy is expelled.

I knew I was getting very cold and began to hurt, but I stuck with it and—after about three hours—I started feeling warm.

Hey, this is pretty nice, I thought.

I didn't know what was going on. I'd never experienced anything like it. It was a nice feeling, being so warm after being so cold. I was burning the sheet piling flush with the concrete floor of the pump cell. It was awkward to burn the piling flush with the concrete. I began to think it would be easier if I could just sit down and burn about two feet off the concrete, so I sat down and started burning at that elevation. It was much easier. That's not what the job required, but I couldn't think backward or forward—I had no sense of past or future. I was living in the immediate time.

I was in scuba and did not have a communication line to the work deck where Louie was tending me. When my shift was over, Louie began pulling on the line to the torch. That was interesting. I saw my hand rise with the torch. I thought, *I can't work without a torch, so I might as well go up with it.*

That decision saved my life. If I had let go and continued to sit on the concrete, I could have died down there.

Louie reached down by the boarding ladder and picked up the torch line. I knew enough to go up the ladder, but was otherwise on autopilot. Louie gave me a hand, got me on deck, and started removing my dive gear. When he headed for the warming shack, I followed. In the shack the oil stove was going full blast. Louie helped me out of my wet suit. All this time I was like an animal, acting on instinct, and following Louie. I got dressed while Louie loaded the dive gear into his truck. My actions looked normal, so he had no idea I was into full-blown hypothermia.

I got in the truck and we headed for Portland, about 45 minutes away. Louie's truck heater was going full blast. After a while, my jaw started jerking and I couldn't control it—I was afraid my teeth would break. By the time we got to Portland, I could talk. I was hurting from the cold, but coming out of the hypothermia.

The next day, Louie could see what I'd done.

"What the hell were you doing, Ken?" he asked.

By this time, I knew what I'd done, too. All I said was, "Just go back where I left off on the concrete and finish it."

Chapter 22: Oregon Coast Drill Platform

ONE DAY FRED Devine received a call for a couple of divers to do some repair on a drilling platform ten miles offshore out of Gearhart, Oregon. Keith Wilson, my log salvage partner, and I drove to Gearhart and caught a helicopter ride out to the drill rig. Even on a day with no wind, the seas on the Oregon Coast can be high. We landed and went to the Superintendent's office. He told us briefly what the job consisted of, and suggested we check in and get a room on the rig, saying, "It's too rough to dive and you may be here for a while."

I suggested we go out and look at the problem and the sea conditions.

We needed to replace broken rigging on the outer side of a thirty-foot-diameter pontoon about twenty feet below the surface. The broken lines were suspender lines the supply boat tied up to when it brought stores and equipment to the rig; it was important it be fixed as soon as possible.

In the water we would be at the mercy of the swell as it tugged on the heavy cables we needed to reconnect—there wouldn't be anything to hang on to except the pad eyes welded to the pontoons. We looked over the situation. I got Keith aside and asked him if he thought he could remove the broken rigging under these rough conditions. He thought he could, and I thought if he could do that, then I'd be able to attach the new rigging.

I went to the Superintendent and explained that we were ready to try the job now. We suited up and Keith went in first. The swells were big and Keith started to feel sick, but was able to remove the broken gear. When it was my turn, I had to attach two new two-inch diameter steel cables with sockets that went between the two large pad eyes and then slip a huge pin through it all. I had to do this two times, all the time flying around with the sea swells. After a struggle, I succeeded. We completed the job that afternoon, flew back to Gearhart, and drove home.

Several weeks later we got another call from the same rig. They requested Devine's send out the same two divers that came last time. Keith and I headed out again. We flew out to the rig, but this time the ocean was flat and clear and conditions were beautiful. The Super' explained what he wanted—we were to look over several anchor shivs, check cables to anchors, plus a couple of minor things. He suggested that we both suit up and do the inspection together. It was a one-man job and I thought it odd he wanted us both in the water.

As we were swimming around enjoying ourselves in these wonderful conditions, I was thinking, *From the surface a person can look down and see what we're doing.* I realized he didn't really need us to do the inspection in the water—he could have done the inspection from the catwalk.

After we dressed, we went to the Super's office to make our report. I asked him why he had us come out. He grinned and replied, "I just wanted to know I could get you two back when I needed to. I've been on these rigs most of my life all over the world and have never known divers that could do what you two do." It was a nice compliment.

Chapter 23: Oil Rig Ways

ONE OF THE JOBS that came Devine's way was for American Pipe, a company building offshore drilling platform rigs in Vancouver, Washington. We poured concrete for the dead man anchors—permanent anchors made out of 120 yards of concrete that were difficult to move. We rebuilt the ways, did all the construction, and then were on site for the launchings.

In order to launch the oil rigs after they were built, American Pipe had to build a series of wooden launching ramps or ways. Literally thousands of piles were driven into the bottom of the Columbia River: A set of three piles a foot or two apart, called a bent, a gap of eight to ten feet, followed by another bent. This went on for 200 to 300 feet into the river. Our job was to cut the piles at grade to fit the launching ramps. Some of the cuts were near the bottom of the river and some were eight feet off the bottom.

Fred Devine showed up to the job site and he was going to run the job. I was there with Keith Wilson and a couple of the hardhat divers. Fred gave us this lecture. "Now boys, here's the deal." He was talking out of one corner of his mouth with a cigarette stuck in the other corner. "We are going to do this all in hardhat, just like it was in World War II."

Oh, shit. Doing it Fred's way was not a problem for the old hard hat divers, but Keith and I weren't too keen on the idea; it would be difficult to shimmy up the piles using hard hat gear. In my mind, I could see that swimming would be much easier. The pay was good and we wanted to work for Devine's. We put on hard hats.

Here we were, weighed down in hardhat gear and using heavy air-powered chain saws in dark, murky water. We had to cut the piles off even with a ledger board nailed to the piles. The two hardhat divers started the job; it took them hours to cut one bent—that was three cuts out of thousands. Fred was all upset. He was pacing the beach and confused that it was going so slow. I knew we could do it faster with scuba.

I told him, "Fred, let me try it."

By now he had had time to get softened up to the idea and told me to give it a shot.

The water was black. I wrapped my legs around a piling and made a cut. I couldn't see the next piling—the visibility was only a couple of feet and the next piling was about eight feet away. To get to it, I stood up on the ledger board atop the piling I'd just cut, and, with the heavy chain saw in my hands, jumped off, and—kicking as hard as I could—hit the next piling and cut it off.

I cut a 200-foot row of pilings on one tank of air. I came up and there were logs floating everywhere. Our crew and the construction crew building the ways were scurrying around in skiffs collecting logs and taking them to the beach.

The ways, large laminated beams for the oil rigs to ride over as they slid into the water, were built on the beach by another company. Keith and I were to connect the finished sections of the ways to the piles, but slight variances in the distance between piles began to add up and the connection points built on land did not perfectly match the piles in the water. It was much harder to fix the problem than to do it right the first time. I proposed to the project manager that Keith and I build the ways in the water. This did not please the ways contractor, but everyone eventually agreed, and the process was faster and more accurate.

American Pipe, our customer, had a young German engineer, Erik, who was designing the ways. When they tried to launch the first oil rig, they discovered that, somehow, one of the other divers screwed up on a dive and it was going to cost the customer a lot of time and money to fix it.

Erik came to me and said, "I want to hire you and Keith to do my diving."

Keith and I were independent divers working for Fred Devine Diving and Salvage Co. on an on-call basis.

"Erik, if I do that," I explained, "I've cut my throat with Devine's. I think there's a better way to do it. Why don't you hire us through Devine's and I promise you Keith and I will do all the dives."

Erik eventually gave in, but said, "I want you and Keith here 24 hours a day during each launch."

Each launch took several days and there were several launches scheduled.

By this time, Devine's had enough work again to have a legitimate office. I called the secretary, Marilyn, Mick's sister-in-law, and told her not to book Keith or me for anything else.

Soon after making the agreement with Erik to do all the dives, Keith and I were finishing our eight-hour shift and here came the hardhat divers. Erik saw them and came running toward me, "I thought you said you were going to do all the dives!"

"Don't worry. I'll take care of it," I reassured him.

I had to tell those two old guys that the only way I could save this job was to be there fulltime; this upset them a bit. After the launch, Keith and I went back to the office with our diary and daily job reports so Marilyn could do the billing.

The mood of the office was cold. Mick said, "Sounds like there's been some back stabbing going on here."

I confronted Mick and told him they had lost the work due to an error by another diver and I saved it by making the arrangement for Keith and me to be there. Mick and the others eventually got over it, to the point that when I quit Devine's a little over nine years later they offered me a share in the company.

Chapter 24: The Greek Freighter

THE FIRST salvage job that started to put Devine's back on the map involved a freighter carrying a cargo of bagged fertilizer headed for Portland that went hard aground on Clatsop Spit.

Dick Barney, the owner of a camera shop in Oregon City, wrote an article about it called Men Against the Sea, published by Popular Mechanics in December 1971.

Men Against the Sea

Breakers 20 feet high sweep in from the Pacific, crashing on sandy shoals that line the mighty Columbia River's mouth. Just the sight of this twisting channel, where seas are whipped to a froth by gusty winds and driven by swift-flowing tidal currents, unsettles even veteran mariners.

When the Captayannis S. ran hard aground on Clatsop Spit that Sunday night— Oct. 22, 1967—she became the 24th major victim of this Oregon-coast graveyard for ships. A Coast Guard distress message signaled the start of a nine-day battle to rescue the freighter and its cargo from total destruction. The 2037-ton, Norwegian-built vessel was on its first voyage under Greek ownership, bound for Portland with her hold full of sacked herring-meal protein concentrate.

A Columbia River bar pilot alerted Capt. Reino Mattila aboard the Salvage Chief, a 192-foot LSM (Landing Ship Medium) converted for salvage work by Fred Devine Diving and Salvage Co. Mattila relayed the alarm to salvage foreman J. H. (Mick) Leitz at the firm's Portland headquarters, then churned full ahead to the scene of the stranding. Now abandoned, but with her deck lights still burning, the ship was easy to find. Trapped in a sand pocket, she was being lifted and slammed against the shallow bottom by each passing swell. The Chief dropped anchor to await Mick Leitz and daylight.

Ninety miles upstream at Portland, Mick alerted the rest of his salvage team. He called Ken Dye, a professional diver, to be his right-hand man, and leased a 12E Hiller helicopter and pilot.

Next morning Mick and Ken boarded the grounded, unmanned ship by dropping from the copter onto an awning atop the aft deckhouse.

A survey revealed that, although the ship was still tight and dry, the after engine-room bulkhead had buckled, binding the propeller shaft so that she couldn't move under her own power. And to make the situation worse, two of her three electric generators were inoperative.

Mick decided to haul the dead ship off with the Chief's powerful engines and winches. First they'd fix the Chief in position with two six-ton salvage anchors set well ahead at angles, then run two steel tow-lines to the freighter. It should be a routine refloating job, Mick figured.

Soon the helicopter dropped the end of a nylon line from the Chief to the two men on the Captayannis S. They passed it through a forward chock and took several turns around one drum of the electric anchor windlass. Switching on the windlass, they heaved in the nylon messenger with a 1¾-inch steel cable attached to its end. As the heavy cable sagged into the watery 1000-foot gap between the two vessels, cross-currents swept it sideways into a wide curve. The windlass slowed down, then stopped; apparently it wasn't developing full power.

Mick will tell you that in the salvage business you don't go out there to see if a job can be done; you go out there to do it. If one thing fails, you try another. You improvise, you jury rig, you make things work.

They ran the line from the anchor windlass drum to the drum of a cargo winch. By operating windlass and winch in tandem—so that the two shared the load—they soon heaved one end of the towline cable aboard. Making the stiff steel cable fast to the ship's mooring bits took time and muscle. Normally it's a job for three or four deckhands, but the two salvage men managed to bend the wire into figure eights unaided.

As they heaved the second towline toward the stricken ship, a strong ebb tide swung the Chief out of the channel, causing her to bump bottom. While the Chief's crew winched her back to deep water, sand closed over part of the towline as it lay on the bottom. When Mick and Ken resumed heaving, they couldn't budge the line.

They added winches to their chain of turning drums until they had five pulling at once. To keep the drums turning at the same speed, they sprinted back and forth to the widely separated winch controls—not an easy stunt on a deck slanted at a 14° angle and coated with fuel oil.

Progress was slow: It was almost midnight when they finally made the second towline fast. They'd been up since dawn and worked hard for 14 hours straight.

Mick and Ken treated themselves to hot showers, then set watches to take soundings every two hours.

Dawn of the second day brought helpers from the Chief, followed through the day by pumps, suction hose, and other gear. Then the Chief shifted her anchorage farther out to try to drag the Captayannis S. across 2000 feet of shoals, through breakers, and the generator quit, leaving the ship pitch black and totally without electric power. Mick and Ken now believed she was structurally damaged beyond economical repair.

Working under the usual "no cure—no pay" contract, their incentive to keep trying was the cargo alone; it still lay largely undamaged in the holds. But with the seas periodically sweeping over the deck, hatches could not safely be opened, nor could a lighter come alongside to take off the cargo. To save the cargo they'd have to save the ship—the two were inseparable.

The shock each time the ship was slammed against the bottom reached the men wherever they were. But in the engine room—right above the point of impact—the effect was strongest. Ladders buckled, stanchions flexed and metal plates fell from overhead catwalks.

Particularly hard jolts fractured bolts that anchored the big diesel engine. The bolts parted with a crack as loud as a rifle shot. But the salvage men had to work in the engine room regardless of the danger.

Dawn of the third day brought moderated winds, though a heavy ground swell continued. A replacement for the Chief's lost anchor arrived by tugboat. The helicopter was now making up for lost time while it was grounded for high winds; it lowered cargo nets filled with pumps and suction hoses, portable light plants and floodlights, oxygen and acetylene tanks, gasoline cans and other gear to the wreck's deck.

The ship's generator had overheated and stopped the day before because of a sand-clogged heat exchanger. They solved this problem by using a gasoline-powered pump, connected to a hose hanging from the vessel's side into the sea, to run sand-free saltwater through the heat exchanger. Once again they had ship's power, which meant electricity for lights, the anchor windlass and cargo winches.

Before dark of the third day, they had one towline back in place and before noon of the fourth, the second one. The Chief would pull only during slack water, they now decided, since the strain on anchors and cables was too great with the current working against both vessels. To hold the wreck steady during tidal current flow, they hooked a line from one of the Chief's after winches to the wreck's port anchor and pulled it out as far as the anchor chain would reach. Then they slacked off on the line and let the anchor dig in.

All this was accomplished none too soon. Throughout the fourth day the wind increased. By 8:00 a.m. of the fifth day it was again near hurricane force. The wreck's deck was awash, so that even the heaving in of the anchor chain to keep it tight was an adventure.

Breakers battered the deckhouse, testing every porthole. High combers put green water over the bridge. The latch gave way on a steel storm door, exposing the two-inch-thick oak inner door to the seas. It soon was smashed to slivers and the deckhouse passageway flooded. Ken managed to get a line through the steel door's handle and around a bracket inside. With the storm door secured, they set up a portable pump to dry out the deckhouse.

The high seas also fouled the sea-suction hose, causing the generator to again overheat and stop. Mick and Ken went on deck to make repairs. Dog-tired and groggy from lack of sleep, they were not too alert. Mick, struggling with the suction line, his back to the sea, never saw the big wave coming. Ken glimpsed it just in time to fling his arms around a vent pipe and hang on.

When the wave had passed, Ken spotted Mick 40 feet away in a tangle of rope, blood running down his face. Ken radioed the Chief and soon Mick was aboard a Coast Guard cutter, on his way to Astoria, Ore., to get a three-inch gash over his right eye sewed up.

Ken gave up on the suction line. He switched back to the ship's pumps to cool the heat exchanger, figuring that sandy water would have to do the job for a while. The thing was to keep the ship's bilge pumps working until they could bring more portable pumps aboard from the Chief. It had become a grim battle to keep the freighter afloat.

That night the Coast Guard insisted for the first time that all hands leave the wreck.

On the morning of the sixth day, with Mick back in action, the salvage men were dismayed to find the main deck awash on the port side. Even worse, the engine room was flooded. Doggedly they went to work pumping out the engine room, using pumps in tandem. Their morale hit bottom when the water level dropped to expose a deep layer of sand covering the engine room floor. Sand pumps were flown from the Chief and put to work.

With the storm still raging that night, all hands again left the wreck.

The seventh day was a replay of the sixth. Water and sand had to be pumped from the engine room. The wreck's piping was generally damaged or inaccessible, yet three of the four holds had to be pumped out if the cargo was to be saved. The answer for No. 1 hold was a suction fitting through its forward bulkhead, from the forepeak tank. No. 2 was tapped through the engine room's forward bulkhead, and they tapped into a usable line to No. 4.

The winds were moderating, but the groundswell continued heavy, cresting as high as 18 feet. The main engine was now loose and rocking on its bed; only the manifold piping kept it upright as the ship pitched.

While the salvage crew fought to keep the wreck from digging its grave in the sandy bottom, the Chief strained to pull her across the shoal. On the eighth day the salvage men could measure the progress toward deep water by watching the freighter's anchor chain. The tighter the chain got, the closer the freighter was to freedom.

The ninth day brought a higher tide and some gain in the battle to keep the wreck afloat. Finally, at 11:20 a.m., Tuesday, Oct. 31, 1967, the Captayannis S. floated free!

For the first time ever, Clatsop Spit had been cheated of a big prize.

There were no cheers, no one handing out medals for valor—just the feeling of satisfaction that comes with a job well done. For the first time in nine days, Mick Leitz, Ken Dye and Capt. Mattila and his crew could look forward to an evening of rest. ***

The *Captayannis S.* aground on Clatsop Spit (October 24, 1967)
Photo by Oregonian photographer, Devine Diving collection

That ship never should have gone aground. The Greek crew had evidently come out of the mountains and this was the Greek captain's first commission. He decided to cross the Columbia River bar (one of the most treacherous in the world) without a bar pilot.

It was interesting working with them. The mate was about six-foot-six and the captain about five-five. We called them Mutt and Jeff.

The mouth of the Columbia River, which separates the states of Oregon and Washington, is a couple of miles wide and dotted with numerous shoals. In the middle of the river birds can stand knee deep in water a mile from shore; even in shallow water silt in the water makes it difficult to see bottom. At its mouth, the Columbia's dredged shipping channel is along the deeper, Oregon side of the river. The navigation channel is marked with a series of numbered buoys—even-numbered red buoys on the southern Oregon side (coming in from the sea, "red right returning") and green odd-numbered markers or buoys on the left side of the channel. When the *Captayannis S.* came into the mouth of the Columbia, the captain misinterpreted Buoy 12 for Buoy 14. Buoy 14 has a right hand turn and Buoy 12 keeps ships off Clatsop spit. Instead of going straight, the *Captayannis S.* turned at buoy 12, right into Clatsop Spit. At that point, they were one of 54 major vessels to go aground on Clatsop Spit. None had ever come off.

Mick Leitz and I went out to the floundering ship by helicopter as the Coast Guard was removing the crew members. We hired George, the second engineer, a young Greek fellow who could speak English, to help us prepare the ship for salvage.

Mick, George and I worked on the *Captayannis S.* for about a week and a half. The incoming seawater suctions for engine cooling were on the bottom of the vessel, which was now in the sand, so we closed the valves and lashed a six-inch pipe overboard for engine room generator cooling. The weather was particularly bad that month. One night, a big storm broke the lashing and the pipe started swinging loose.

To keep the generators running, we had to re-secure the cooling water pipe. Mick went out on deck ahead of me; I was right behind him. A two-story house was in the center of the ship; cargo loading hatches and booms were located on the main deck forward and aft of the house; and lifeboats were strapped in bunks on either side of the house on the boat deck, the first deck above the main deck. I had taken only a couple steps onto the main deck and was going past the aft cargo mast, a three-foot-diameter pipe, when I sensed something and looked up. A huge wave, well higher than the two-story house above me, was preparing to break over the ship.[17] I'd never seen anything like it and I didn't have time to yell. All I could do was swing my arms around the mast and hang on. The wave crest towered above the twenty-foot-tall house. It came down directly into one of the beautiful twenty-four-foot wood plank life boats on the upper deck and shattered it.

A piece of the shattered lifeboat hit Mick in the head and cut him pretty bad; it may have knocked him out. Heavy green water washed over the entire length of the ship. The bulwarks created a four-foot-deep pool of cold seawater, filling the aft end of the ship. We couldn't do anything until the water drained out the

---

[17]Rogue waves. In oceanography, they are more precisely defined as waves whose height is more than twice the significant wave height (SWH), which is itself defined as the mean of the largest third of waves in a wave record. Therefore rogue waves are not necessarily the biggest waves found at sea; they are, rather, surprisingly large waves for a given sea state. Rogue waves seem not to have a single distinct cause, but occur where physical factors such as high winds and strong currents cause waves to merge to create a single exceptionally large wave. http://en.wikipedia.org/wiki/Rogue_wave

A sneaker wave is a disproportionately large coastal wave that can sometimes appear in a wave train without warning. The terminology itself is popular rather than scientific: there is no scientific coverage (or evidence) of the phenomenon as a distinct sort of wave with respect to height or predictability—like there is on other extreme wave events such as rogue waves. Because they are much larger than preceding waves, sneaker waves can catch unwary swimmers, washing them out to sea. It is not uncommon for people walking or standing on beaches and ocean jetties to also be washed into the sea. Sneaker waves are mainly referred to in warnings and reports of incidents for the coasts of Northern California, Oregon and Washington in the United States. These sneaky waves also occur on the west coast of Canada, they are commonly seen in Tofino and Ucluelet. http://en.wikipedia.org/wiki/Sneaker_wave

scuppers. Mick was tangled in a mooring line up against the bulwark and looked about to be washed overboard. I ran to Mick and pulled him back, then radioed for a helicopter to take him off the freighter to the hospital. (Note: The Coast Guard cutter Dick mentioned in the article would not have been able to make it out there in those conditions.)

It was the worst injury we had in the ten years I worked for Devine's. [18]

---

[18] *Captayannis S.* During a violent storm on October 22, the Greek freighter *Captayannis S.*, a small four-hold vessel of 4,570 tons, built in 1946, was swept ashore on Clatsop Spit at the south entrance to the Columbia River. Her master reported a faulty radio prevented his calling a bar pilot and he approached Clatsop Spit to signal one. The 22 crew members, including two women, were removed by Coast Guard helicopters. The following day six of the ship's deck and engineering officers were put back aboard to assist in salvage efforts by the Astoria-based salvage vessel Salvage Chief, which pulled her free after eight days in the breakers. Part of her cargo of fish meal, which been loaded in Norway for discharge at Portland and Olympia, was removed after her arrival at Portland and reprocessed for poultry and stock feed. The cost of repairs proved greater than the value of the ship and she was eventually sold for scrap for less than $20,000. Gordon Newell, Maritime Events of 1967, H. W. McCurdy Marine History of the Pacific No.
http://www.cimorelli.com/cgi-
bin/magellanscripts/ship_dates_volume.asp?ShipName=Captayannis+S
For info re: legal action taken, see: Civ. No. 67-568. United States District Court D. Oregon. November 10, 1969.
http://www.leagle.com/xmlResult.aspx?xmldoc=19691172306FSupp866_11024.xml&docbase=
CSLWAR1-1950-1985\

Chapter 25: The Zenith of Salvage Operations

WHEN DEVINE'S got an emergency call to rescue a brand-new Japanese logging ship aground in Grays Harbor in Aberdeen, Washington, Mick Leitz and I quickly chartered a plane and flew up. The grounded ship was fully loaded with logs headed back to Japan. When we arrived at the site, about eighty miles north of the mouth of the Columbia River, the tide was going out. That first tide was not that bad of a drop, but the tide would come back in again, and the next tide a few hours later would be a drastic low tide.

The stern of the ship, which drew less water than the center and bow, was hanging out over deep water; only the deeper front two-thirds of the vessel was aground in the sandy mud. We believed if the ship went through the next low tide that the stern would no longer be supported by the water and the weight of the unsupported stern would break the back of the ship. Our goal was to get the ship afloat before the next low tide.

At the same time that Mick and I were on our way to the site, the *Salvage Chief* sailed from Astoria. While we waited for the *Salvage Chief* to arrive, Mick and I started the process of rigging the freighter for pulling gear. When the *Salvage Chief* arrived, we got our gear aboard and started rigging. It was hard work getting heavy cables, cable straps for wrapping mooring bits, cable clamps, and all that ready for the *Salvage Chief*.

We were able to pull the Japanese ship off with the high tide and save it from the real low tide. The *Salvage Chief* towed the freighter to Portland to put it in dry dock for repairs.

Before the insurers would allow the ship to sail again, the prop had to be repaired and a full bottom survey completed, but the weight of the cargo was too much to lift the hull all the way out of the water in the dry dock. The owners wanted to sail the next day. With a partial lift, and by rotating the prop, we could get one bent blade at a time high enough out of the water to repair it, and we could do the bottom survey from underwater.

We got our crew together for the survey. It was nighttime and the ship was partially in the water; in order to see we had headlamps on our masks. Using come-alongs, we strung eighth-inch cable under the ship at each frame station. Then the divers went under and measured the setup at each frame station and between frame stations. We surfaced and reported, from memory, the condition of each section to someone recording it on the surface. For hours we went back and forth, diving, measuring, resurfacing, and reporting. Mick used the information to make a grid of the bottom showing the measurements for the setups.

By morning the survey was complete and the prop faired. The underwriters looked at our survey and approved the vessel to sail. There was little time lost from the original sail date. Once the logs were taken off in Japan, the Japanese company's surveyors took the ship out of the water and used transits and levels to validate the work we had done underwater in the dark. The results matched perfectly. The Japanese surveyors sent a letter to express their appreciation.

When a salvage company does a job like this, the job is done under what is called a "Lloyd's Open Form,"[19] which is a salvage contract developed over a hundred years ago. In essence, it states that a formal contract does not need to be signed, that time is of the essence, you do your best to salvage the vessel, and make a report on your efforts describing the dangers, risks, effort required, etc. The report goes to Lloyd's of London. A Lloyd's arbitration board of people skilled in the world of salvage reviews the report and makes a monetary award. Pretty soon you get a check in the mail. Sometimes it's good, sometimes not so good.

Before I started working for Devine, they had done something that didn't put them in good stead with the underwriters, mainly Lloyd's of London, the primary insurer for ships and cargo. I was aware of the friction, but never knew the cause. We had no way to know in advance how well we would come out on this job.

In this case, because of the short amount of time we spent, we thought Lloyd's awarded us more than we thought we'd earned (I think it was $75,000), but we'd

---

[19] A Lloyd's Open Form, formally Lloyd's Standard Form of Salvage Agreement, but more commonly referred to as LOF, is a standard legal document for a proposed marine salvage operation. The two-page contract is published by Lloyd's of London. It is called "open" because it is literally open, with no amount of money being stipulated for the salvage job: the sum to be paid is determined later in London by a professional arbitrator. At the top of page one, beneath the title "Salvage Agreement" is a statement of the contract's fundamental premise. "NO CURE – NO PAY". The form originated in the late 19th century and is the most common such form of international salvage agreement. The arbitrator, who is invariably a Queen's Counsel practicing (sic) at the Admiralty Bar, follows the English law of civil salvage, in determining the salvage award. The value of the ship, its cargo and freight at risk are taken into account when the arbitrator decides what the award should be, together with the extent of the dangers and the difficulty in effecting the salvage. http://en.wikipedia.org/wiki/Lloyd's_Open_Form

saved the ship, saved the cargo, and got it sailing again almost immediately and that was worth a lot to the ship's owners. Lloyd's sent a nice letter with the check. It said, essentially, "Gentlemen, We know that you will be pleased with your award. We know it is more than we would normally award for this type of operation. You are to be commended because you have performed the zenith of salvage operations."

It was another high point of diving for Devine's.

The *Salvage Chief* in foreground, Grays Harbor, Washington (date unknown)
Devine Diving collection. This is a good example of the conditions in which Ken and the crew lived and worked, sometimes for weeks at a time.

Chapter 26: Dutch Guiana

EARLY IN MY career with Devine's, the Lloyd's representative on the West Coast said they had a ship sink off the east coast of South America, in a remote part of Dutch Guiana (officially called Suriname).

The ship sank in a very, very isolated jungle area, which made the incident look a bit suspicious, and Lloyd's wanted us to check it out and see if there was anything going on that shouldn't be.

The ship was owned by a Greek shipping company that owned about a dozen ships. Each year, for about three years, the Greek company lost a ship, but it was always the ship at the tail end of the line—it was never one of the better ships—and the shipping company was collecting the insurance.

We got acquainted with the Dutch harbor master at Paramaribo, who furnished a vessel to take us out to the sunken ship. I rigged up a welder/generator to burn a hole in the side of the ship to gain direct access to the engine room; the ship was too big to hunt around looking for the engine room using a scuba tank.

We figured the only way for a ship to sink as fast as this one had sunk was to break the main sea chest that brought sea cooling water to the engines; I wanted to go into the engine room see if the huge valve on one side of the sea chest had been removed.

The operation never got to that point. When we flew our equipment to Paramaribo, my dive compressor got lost. We waited a week for it to arrive. Next, the conditions were bumpy and everyone not in the water got sick. I was fine, but everyone else was miserable.

It was tropical, it was hot, and the surf was breaking over the sunken vessel. I made a survey of the wreck, figured out what had to be done, and what equipment I needed. The vessel we were on was riding the surf alongside the sunken vessel, which was just underwater—if our anchor gave way, our vessel would end up on the back of the wreck. Even worse, we were a long ways from a harbor—if a storm blew up or we needed assistance of any kind, we were in jeopardy. Given the conditions, the underwriter decided we had to give it up.

Looking at the whole picture, it was probably the right thing to do. It was an adventure to go to South America on a diving job for Lloyd's, but it was frustrating to never prove if the ship had been scuttled.

Chapter 27: Tunnel Vision

WHILE DIVING for Devine's, Keith and I continued to run our log salvage operation. One day I was running the tug boat up the river to get a load of logs and my mind wandered to the first time the voice spoke to me saying, "You are going to be a professional diver."

All the time I was diving until now—between 1960 and 1969 doing log salvage and then heavy marine salvage—I was aware the message I heard when I was nine years old was coming true, I was a professional diver, but I had been too busy to think about it too deeply.

It was an awakening. That was when I started looking at the spiritual side of life more closely.

That night I lay in bed, thinking this through, and thought, *Well, if there's an entity that can tell me at the age of nine what I'm going to be, why can't I look into the future and see what it holds? I wonder how we tap that source?*

All of a sudden, I had a vision. No voice, just a vision. I was looking down a tunnel, and the tunnel represented my life. There were no words, nothing absolute. It was just a tunnel and I could see a diving career ahead of me, nothing specific, but down a ways was a block in the tunnel. I knew the tunnel went on, but there was a block in the vision and a change. I couldn't see beyond the block, but I could sense a change. I didn't feel that it was the end of my diving career, but I also couldn't see what it meant. It was weird.

Six years later, I had almost more change than I could handle.

Chapter 28: Keith Quits Diving

KEITH AND I were always very busy working, but we had time to dream up other schemes, too.

One of the ideas we had when working for Troxell in Pasco was to design and build the first commercial underwater submarine, something we could incorporate into our dive operation. In our off time, we learned about pressure on steel, designed the sub, drew up plans, and went to an engineering company in Spokane, Washington, to finalize the design and build the sub, but never had enough money to put our idea into action. We never completed the project, but the hope and concept of having a small sub for deep water was a great dream; as far as we knew, there were none in existence.

Instead, Keith and I built an eight-plex together and two four-plexes separately. From 1965 to 1969, Keith and I stayed with Devine's, filling in when they needed on-call divers, and building apartments the rest of the time. One day I sat down with Keith to add up the numbers. We came to the conclusion that if a guy kept doing this, he could get rich. Therefore, Keith surprised me when he announced, "Ken, I've made my last professional dive."

"What do you mean? We have the world at our feet." I couldn't understand why he would want to change anything.

"I don't care," he said.

Perhaps Keith was thinking of how miserable the jobs were, such as working on the Mossyrock dam, where we were hardhat diving in 180' of water on mixed air—we'd work at depth for five minutes, then spend two hours decompressing.

Dive work was often dangerous. The stop logs (steel gates that came down to stop the

Keith Wilson and his mother aboard a Chris Craft he and Ken salvaged (circa 1965)

water flow) in the deepest area of a dam we worked on were leaking. We stuffed the leaks with a baloney tube (burlap stuffed into a sock). The water leaving the dammed lake created suction; if we weren't careful, it would suck our hoses in, too, keeping us there forever.

On a project at Tongue Point near the mouth of the Columbia River, Keith was working under a ship that had hit a log or other debris. Before the ship could sail again, the insurance company required the captain obtain a seaworthy certificate, which required divers to feel the entire bottom of the ship by hand and report their findings to the Captain. Keith was under the ship when the tide changed and the ship started to shift; the water was shallow and Keith was pushed down into the mud as the huge ship dragged across his body.

Keith Wilson and Ken Dye Scappoose, Oregon (2012) Still close friends—and still breathing—50 years later

Perhaps he thought of the other times he almost died. Once Keith ran out of air cleaning out the spillways for a hydroelectric dam. A dam may have five or six spillways and you may have to go through a compartment or around a wall to get there, it isn't always a straight shot and you don't necessarily know exactly where you are when something goes wrong, making it tricky to get back to the surface in a hurry. Because it could get sucked into a pump, we didn't always use a lanyard to mark our route. And we had a bad habit of diving until we were out of air; in those days we didn't carry reserve air and we always pushed our time in the water to the edge. Keith eventually came out of the spillway, but at the time you don't know you are going to make it until you do.

One time we went down to Coos Bay to put a patch on a cargo ship that hit a log out at sea; the impact created a leak. We had to bolt on a patch and Keith was working inside, down through six or seven hatches, when he ran out of air. Normally, we would follow the light filtering down from the surface, but Keith was down too deep in the ship's hold for surface light to reach and he wasn't using a tag line—he had to feel his way out. He held his breath and told himself to calm down and think his way through it. Pretty soon, he saw the light and followed it up.

Many of the salvage jobs were emergencies and Keith got three speeding tickets in one month racing from one job to the other.

Plus, Keith's wife, Linda, was pregnant with their second child. He figured, *There's got to be a better life.* He was diving for Devine, selling real estate, and building. It was too much. He decided, *It's time to get my head out of the water.*

At that moment, Keith committed fully to building apartments and houses in Clackamas County and did very well. He is still doing it to this day. His wife, Linda, is the manager. She's a wonderful lady, a great supporter and wife. She kiddingly "complains" how she does the dirty work of collecting rent and evicting tenants while Keith plays at building apartments and developing property. They are a great team.

Personally, I wanted to keep diving, but I was also looking at developing Sportcraft Landing—we always looked to the future.

Chapter 29: Sportcraft Landing

ONE DAY—when Keith and I were still running our log salvage operations on the Willamette River—we brought our barge down through the locks to the lower Willamette and tied up at Sportcraft Landing for the night. That's when I met Ruth and Clair Huff for the first time. Like us, Clair had a log patrol license from the State, which gave us something in common. After that, when we needed to repair the log salvage barge we hauled out at Sportcraft.

Willamette Falls at Oregon City.
The Willamette Falls is a natural waterfall on the Willamette River between Oregon City and West Linn, Oregon, in the United States. It is the largest waterfall in the American Pacific Northwest by volume, and the seventeenth widest in the world.- Horseshoe in shape, it is 1,500 feet (460 m) wide and 40 feet (12 m) high with a flow of 30,849 cu ft/s (874 m³/s), located 26 miles (42 km) upriver from the Willamette's mouth. Until 2011 a canal and set of locks allowed vessels to pass into the main Willamette Valley. Those locks are now closed. http://en.wikipedia.org/wiki/Willamette_Falls

At the start of what became to be known as the 1964 Christmas flood, when the current was beginning to run really hard, we were salvaging logs in front of Sportcraft. I could feel the current getting stronger, so I came up from my dive to tell Keith to get above the falls as quick as possible, or he wouldn't be able to get up to Publishers with our load. Shortly after that, they (the Army Corps of Engineers) shut down the locks.

Keith and I came back from our log landing above the falls to help the Huffs tie lines from the docks and buildings to cottonwood trees to keep the moorage from drifting away. At the time, the Huffs had one wood dolphin (a set of three piles driven into the river bottom and tied or bolted together at the top) offshore to tie the moorage off. During the winter, they untied the docks from the dolphin and retied them in the trees on shore.

The 1964 flood—called a 100-year flood—had a high water of 49 feet.[20] Many people don't understand what 49 feet of water below the falls means. I use the story of when Barry Huff caught a steelhead with his hands to help them understand it—the fish got caught up trying to get over a lane divider on McLoughlin Boulevard. At the Oregon City Shopping Center the stores in the middle had basements full of water and water halfway up the walls on the ground floor.

In the beginning, Sportcraft Landing moorage was just basic log docks. When the I-205 Bridge went in at Oregon City, the original design eliminated the access road to the moorage. Clair Huff's wife, Ruth, got the fishermen together to write letters to the governor saying they wanted access to the river.

Governor McCall called and said, "Ruth, call off your dogs. We're going to give you access."

When the bridge was built, the old Boones Ferry barge was parked over by the bank; it laid there and rotted and got into pretty bad shape. Clair had a tiny little tow boat we called the *Judy* boat. It had a little Chrysler Ace, the smallest six cylinder engine they made. Barry, the Huff's son, and Clair got permission to take the ferry; Clair and Barry got it floating high and towed it to Sportcraft Landing. The idea was to put the barge right below the gas dock and build a restaurant. They partially beached the barge and built it up by building up over the old sides. Barry was a carpenter. He and his dad added a large single-story building with a small cabin on top—in the middle and upstairs was a 14'x14' captain's cabin with a spiral staircase and a cot Clair used to take naps. (I later added bunk beds for the

---

[20]Christmas Flood 1964 At Oregon City, Willamette Falls was unrecognizable as a waterfall, and the city was flooded by several feet of water. In Portland, the lower deck of the Steel Bridge was underwater and had also been hit by a log raft consisting of 1,000 logs. The impact of the raft severely damaged the Hawthorne Bridge, closing it for a year. At 12 feet (3.7 m) above flood stage, the flooding of the Willamette River at Portland in 1964 was second only to the 1948 flood that wiped out Vanport City. At its peak, the water was at the top of Downtown Portland's seawall. http://en.wikipedia.org/wiki/Christmas_flood_of_1964

kids). The main level contained a tackle shop, a counter with stools, and a little restaurant.

As I said before, besides log salvage, Keith and I were building apartments—it was very lucrative and Keith decided to give up diving to build apartments fulltime.

I was also making plans.

Clair Huff's father was failing and needed help; Clair and Ruth's plan was to sell Sportcraft and move back to Halfway, Oregon, where they were both born and raised, to take care of Dad Huff. One day I sat on the bluff overlooking Sportcraft Landing, and could see it was going to take a ton of work to make the moorage into what it could be. I assume the spiritual side was moving me. No voice, no vision, just an awareness of final results—a sensation that I didn't need to worry about money, that if I did the right thing, the money would be there when it was needed; that it would work out okay. I was sitting there and thinking of the possibilities— the older fishermen who used Sportcraft relied on it for access to the river, which was their main form of recreation; they couldn't afford anything else.

I consciously thought about money—I could continue building apartments and diving, and become quite wealthy, or I could buy this place and have less money. I decided money wasn't as important as doing what I thought was right. Building that moorage was the right thing. Being wealthy was not as important as being happy and helping other people. I could just see those old guys who used the river and helping them get proper access to their river so they could enjoy it. The Huffs provided the initial access—I felt that if I built more boat slips, even more people would be able to enjoy the river.

In 1969 I implemented the first phase of my plan, sold my apartments, and purchased Sportcraft Landing from Ruth and Clair Huff. I was still diving for Devine's, but finding the money to work on Sportcraft was a real challenge; I couldn't have done it without my income from diving—the income from the existing customers wasn't enough to offset the expense of building for the future. In the purchase I got the barge building, Ruth and Clair's house, the gas dock, and the log float boat docks—Sportcraft catered to small fishing boats, which bow tied to the dock and left the stern trailing out in the current. These minimal facilities were located at the base of Willamette Falls in Oregon City—the most difficult location of any moorage I've ever seen. It will always be a struggle to maintain a moorage here, but providing access to the river is a good thing.

The height of 49 feet of potential water, the height the river reached during the Columbus Day storm in 1964, dictates how everything is installed—it has to withstand extreme high water and a very fast, raging current.

I got some twelve by twelve timbers from a dock Devine's tore down that I bolted together to make the main walkway from the shore outward; I placed the sides of the timbers with rotted spots on the bottom—they wouldn't rot under water. As I added more docks, fingers, slips, buildings and other facilities, I needed a permanent solution to the high water problem; we drove many steel pilings to support the dock system.

Originally, my wife Sandy and our daughter Laurie ran the little restaurant. During salmon season, they got up at three a.m. to feed the fishermen. It was always busy and washing dishes in the low sinks was back-breaking work. After the first year, I brought my parents into the moorage as partners; they had been running a resort in southern California and had the experience I needed. Dad ran the gas pumps and Mom managed the little restaurant.

I was diving for Devine's and occasionally gone for weeks or even months at a time; the money I made diving I reinvested in the moorage.

Besides the improved dock mooring system, we built additional docks, a modern access ramp, a sales building to sell marine supplies the fishermen needed, a new gas dock, a marine repair shop, fishing boat and canoe rentals, and enlarged the snack shop.

My parents were still living at Sportcraft when Mom was in her sixties—she died suddenly one night, probably of a heart attack. Dad lived for several years more. When he got Alzheimer's, my sister, Deanne, took care of him until he died, too. It's hard to lose people you are close to.

I don't have a firm theory about what happens after we die. I've read other people's theories, but that's just information, their feelings. When we die, I think there is another world we go to; we don't take our bodies with us—we become a spiritual being.

After the 1996 flood—the second "100 year" flood in thirty-two years—I went to FEMA and borrowed $89,000 to replace the steel pilings and docks I lost.

When I put the docks and pilings back, I put them back even better and stronger, including tying cables to dolphins (two or more wood or steel pilings driven close together with the tops tied or welded together) on the beach. Most of the vertical piles have one or two batter piles to brace the plumb pile that the docks ride on up and down as the river level changes with the seasons. A river level is affected by rainfall, snowmelt, and storms and minimally or not at all by tides—you can't predict what the level the river is going to be from year to year. Some plumb piles have two or more batter piles to back them up to hold the bigger docks and buildings. In addition to all the dolphins, batter piles, etc., I installed a cable system from the top of each pile that can be tightened independently of each other, with the most upstream dolphin cable tied to another dolphin on the shore. I also installed two anchor dolphins. I've never seen a system like this. It's unique and isn't usually necessary—this kind of robust system is only needed in a place with extreme currents, like we have at Oregon City.

During the period from 1969 to 1980, I figure I invested $1,000,000. I am happy to have been able to provide this access to the river to so many people, but the financial return has been marginal; I realized then I would have to do something other than Sportcraft for my retirement and built two more moorages in another location. More on that later.

Chapter 30: The Killer Snag

As I was going through my life, the log salvage and all that, I never spoke about the spiritual because I was afraid people would make fun of me. I vowed to always tell the truth so people would believe me when I did say something about the spiritual.

There came a point where it was obvious that my life was being spiritually guided—I looked back and clearly saw they had always been there. I was grateful for the benefits I'd been given: I became a successful professional diver and was able to build three moorages. In prayer, I asked, *How can I show my gratitude for what I've been given?*

The voice replied, "People."

The spiritual side is very cautious about the amount of detail they give; they give only the minimum amount of information. I had to figure out what it meant. To me, it meant, "Help people." I had been doing this for a long time, but the voice message was confirmation: I could have kept making good money building apartments; instead, I bought Sportcraft Landing and built it up so more people could have access to the river.

Earlier in life, I was able to provide meat to people who needed it. It seemed the spiritual thought I could do more.

Living on the river brought me into frequent contact with Dean Hartley, the Marine Patrol Officer for Clackamas County. Occasionally, Dean came down to the marina with a long face.

"What's wrong?" I'd ask him.

It might be a drowning, a tree in the channel, or a snag waiting to wreck a boat.

After he told me the problem, I'd say, "Well let's go take a look and see what the situation is," and off we'd go.

One time, someone who worked for the county had a nephew that competed in a white water river raft race on the Santiam River. The family was on the beach cheering them on. This kid saw his family and jumped off the raft and swam over to them. He didn't make it. There was a lot of current and no one knew where the body was. The Santiam River was out of Dean's jurisdiction, but someone who knew what I had done in similar cases asked Dean if I would help. I agreed, adding, "But here's the deal. I don't want a lot of people there. No newspapers. No extra family. All you have to do is show me where you last saw his head."

Someone in the family had a jet boat; I asked them to not follow me. My friend and insurance agent, Bob Wievesick, for whom I'd built a modified A-frame float home at Sportcraft, and I took my old blue Ford dive van. When we got to the scene of the accident, I said, "Bob, this isn't where the body is; the current is too strong. What I'm going to do is weight myself down by five extra pounds."

A drowned body has no air and is heavier than a live one. With the extra weight I was going to replicate a drowned body. A body sinks shortly after drowning and comes up again when gases start to form inside the body, usually in a week or two, depending on the temperature of the water. I was there a day or two after the drowning and that hadn't happened yet.

"I'm going to float down the river. You follow in the van. When I need air, I'll get another tank from the van."

I floated down the river following the bottom; I needed to become the body. When I got to a dead spot in the river, a hole, I laid still until a boil came along and pushed me out. A flowing river isn't consistent, it pushes and pulls. Pretty soon the river spread out and got shallow. The current got slower and slower and slower. Pretty soon, there was the body lying in front of me. I dragged it to the bank and tied it off with a piece of yellow line from the van to the limb of a tree, leaving the body in the water. A truck with one of the family members came along. I told them the boy was at the end of the line. I didn't want to be around when they pulled him out. I didn't want to deal with the family. They want to thank you and get all slobbery and I didn't need that.

In another case, someone was fishing below the falls in Oregon City and drowned. Below the falls is a rock pinnacle in about twenty feet of water. I let my body drop off the end of the rock just like a drowned body would do. There was a hole on the other side of the rock and it was black in there. I fell right into a nest of sturgeon. A sturgeon is a large, prehistoric fish with a hard, scaly body. They beat the shit out of me trying as I worked to get out of the hole. I went to the surface and took my bearings. When I got to shore, I sketched out the spot and gave it to Barry

Huff and told him that's where he could catch sturgeon. The first time he tried he caught a six-foot fish.

Two other situations with the County where Dean came down to Sportcraft with a long face come to mind. The first was a few years before I bought the moorage.

"What's the matter Dean?" I would ask.

During the 1964 flood a huge, huge stump with rocks in the roots came down the Clackamas River. It had been a tree cut down in the woods and the stump was five or six feet in diameter. Large rocks caught in the stump's roots acted like an anchor. The stump sat in the river a few years. When fishermen in drift boats came around the corner of the river, they would encounter a ripple and this tree was right there in the middle. The water on the upstream side of the stump was three or four feet higher than the other side of the stump. A couple of boats flipped over the stump and people drowned.

The hazard got the nickname Killer Stump by the newspapers. The Sheriff didn't like it and put the problem into Dean's lap. I told Dean we could take care of it. I bought some dynamite, primer, and a cap. We got the Sheriff's patrol boat and launched it.

"Now, you run the boat," I told him.

I had my dive suit on and had taken a bundle of six or eight sticks of dynamite, wrapped it with primer cord, and bundled it together with tape, leaving 200 feet of primer cord lying in the bottom of the boat. I had Dean to drive the patrol boat up against the stump, pushing against it. The water was piled up high on either side of the skiff, but the patrol boat was placed in the center of the swell and protected. I dove down to the bottom of the stump and, sure enough, there was a cavity I could shove the dynamite into. I secured the bundle in place with some sticks, came to the surface and got back into the boat. As Dean drove the boat down the river, I fed out the primer cord. At the end of the two hundred feet we set off the dynamite. Because I'd positioned the explosive in the heart of the stump and under water, it blew the rocks out of the stump and blew the stump into two or three pieces that, now free of the rocks, floated down the river.

Another time, a huge Douglas fir on the bluff above the Sandy River fell into the river at a fifteen degree angle; it looked like the tree was growing out of the river upside down. Fishermen in drift boats would come around the river, hit the tree, and people would drown.

"Okay," I told Dean when he asked for my help, "we can take care of that."

I took my chain saw and climbing gear. At about fifteen feet from the water I cut a big wedge in the trunk; I did this two more times moving up the tree. I had Dean lower down some dynamite packages. I placed a package into each V and filled the V with mud. Each package had primer cord. Dean and I went down the river in the boat and shot the dynamite. I can still see it in my mind—three fifteen-foot pieces of log in the air at the same time. They hit the river and floated away.

I was glad to be able to help. As the Marine Patrol Officer for Clackamas County, Dean was the public face on these assignments and got the credit; but when the Sheriff wanted to give Dean a public award, Dean would not accept unless I was included. It was good of him, but it meant having to put on my good clothes and go to the award ceremony.

For a number of years, I picked up bodies all over the area for various counties. After a while, the local Sheriff came to me and said, "Ken, we want you to train a Search and Rescue team."

I agreed, but reluctantly. In my experience, throwing public money at a problem usually didn't make it better. But I went ahead and set up a program and had the Sheriff's divers practice drills. The last dive was a night dive in a search pattern. Afterward, we had a meeting and I asked the guys, "How do you feel about what you just did?"

They responded, "We feel we're not qualified."

That response sums it up, but it didn't stop Search and Rescue teams from forming all across the country. Our Federal government back then (mid 1960s) connected with sheriff departments all over the country and let it be known they wanted to get involved to help fund local programs. One program the Feds came up with included grants to develop Search and Rescue teams. Once that happens and 'free' money is offered, you can't have skilled volunteers using their own equipment, you have to hire people, and buy the latest equipment, and trucks, and boats, and boat houses, and it grows out of control, but now the Federal government has the local sheriff departments by the balls, which is what they wanted in the first place. Where I used to look for bodies for free, now we have these paid guys and their equipment sitting around doing nothing. It's gotten out of hand.

Chapter 31: The Mill was a Disaster

NOT ONLY did Devine's do salvage work on ships, barges, tugs and fishing boats, we worked on dams on the Columbia River, offshore on oil exploration rigs, and offshore pipelines.

This story is about a pipeline job in Eureka, California. There were two big paper companies located there and they had three different pipelines we maintained. We installed one of the pipelines and did the major repairs.

One of the mills scheduled us to fix a pipeline during the Christmas shutdown; we did a lot of work on pipes during the holidays. This pipeline consisted of a four-foot-diameter, wood-stave pipe that came from the mill to the beach, where it changed to a concrete-encased steel pipe that went beyond the surf where effluent was discharged through diffusers at the end of the pipe. The steel portion of the line beyond the surf got a break in it and Devine's was hired to fix it.

For this job, we created an airlock for getting into the pipe by building a diving bell attached to a flange on the concrete and steel section of pipe on the beach. Pressurize the bell, pressurize the pipe, push the water down until it came out the pipe at the break below the surface, and the bubbles would show where the crack was located.

Now, this particular mill was a disaster. The engineering and maintenance people were not competent; it was always dangerous out there for us. We never had trouble with the other mill.

For larger jobs like this, we always had a pre-job conference with Engineering. In the meeting we set out where our responsibility started and left off, and where the mill's started and left off; each group knew what the other was doing and how we were going to coordinate.

Our job was to repair the underwater leak in the concrete-encased steel pipe lying beyond the surf under the ocean surface. First, we had to plug a valve in the wood stave pipe going back to the mill so it wouldn't leak chemicals down to us. We then built an air and liquid-tight dam inside the wood stave pipe so we could blow the remaining liquid out of the concrete section of pipe and keep new liquid from coming down to us from the mill.

There were five of us on the job: Me, my brother Norm, Kent, Larry, and Cliff. Kent Cochran was a professional diver-welder-mechanic that I got into Devine's; Larry was a tender in the bell (he later introduced me to my second wife, Kathy); Cliff was a good guy and wanna-be diver who worked for Devine's, his job was to be outside the bell to supply parts to Norm and Larry. (In a little bit I'll tell you how we almost lost Cliff a few years later working for the same mill.)

Kent and I put on wetsuit bottoms—it was too hot in the pipe for tops. Carrying caulking equipment, we waded up inside the wood stave pipe heading back to the mill. The pipe had a couple of feet of liquid in it, making it half full. One of the responsibilities of the mill was to flush the system of chemicals used to break down wood fiber (chemicals used for paper production include acids/alkalis, lime, sulfurous acid, sodium hydroxide (lye), sodium sulfide) before we went inside the pipe. The head engineer assured us they had flushed all the residue out of the lines with fresh water. There is always some residue, but the head engineer assured us the two feet of liquid remaining in the four-foot pipe was neutralized and perfectly safe for us.

As Kent and I worked on the wood stave portion of the pipe, our skin started to tingle. We finished caulking up the valve then went out of the pipe and up to the medical station in the mill. We had pretty good chemical burns on our legs; our skin was hot and tingled, but didn't blister—it felt like jellyfish stings. The nurse cleaned off our skin and put on some medication that tempered the sting and we went back to work.

I asked the head engineer if there was any other source of liquid between the valve we sealed and where we were going to build the dam. He said not, but just in case promised to man an emergency pump twenty-four hours a day at the hatch midway in the low point of the wood stave pipe. This way, if there were any leaks into the pipe, the liquid would flow to the low point and the pump could take it out. If the water rose to a certain level, the guy watching the pipe was to notify us so we could get out, notify the mill management, and start the pump.

Kent and I built a dam of wood and plastic sheeting designed to withstand inward air pressure from the offshore, downstream side of the pipe. Using large-volume, low-pressure barge blowers hooked to the bell, we pushed an air bubble down the pipe which forced the liquid in the pipe out the end where the break was located. Once the pipe was partially free of seawater, Kent and I crab walked several hundred feet down the pipe to caulk up the crack in the pipe with wet rags, this was a temporary fix which allowed us to force the water further down the steel pipe and dry the area we needed to work on. Once the section of pipe we were working on was free of water, we pulled sheets of steel, welding leads, airline, electrical lines for lighting, and everything else we needed to permanently repair the pipe. We stationed my brother, Norm, in the bell and had an airlock through which he could pass small tools.

The steel sheets were pre-formed to fit the pipe so all we had to do was weld them into place. Kent and I were in the pipe and were about halfway done with the internal patch when I noticed there was water running down the bottom of the pipe. We were wearing wet suit bottoms and sweatshirts. It took a second before I realized how dangerous a situation this placed us in.

I hollered at Kent, "Let's get out of here! The dam is breaking!"

We started running, as best we could inside a four-foot-diameter pipe, several hundred feet back to the diving bell.

As I ducked up to go into the bell, I looked at our dam. We designed it to bulge inward to withstand the air pressure we applied to keep the sea out of the pipe, but now it was bulging outward and water was coming out the bottom of one of the seams in the middle of the dam where the plastic had broken. We slammed the cover to the bell. While we had been inside working on the pipe, outside there was a major downpour. The mill had told us the only access to the pipe was the valve we sealed, but there was another: storm water ran off acres of blacktopped areas and roofs of the mill into drains. All the drains went into a pipe that poured into the big pipe above where we were working. Rain run off was filling the pipe and no one was pumping it out.

There was no shelter over the emergency pump or the man assigned to run it. The pump was an old one with a rope wrapped around a pulley for starting. The rope was soaking wet and the guy assigned to man the pump was wrapping it the wrong direction. He never did get it started. The role was not important to the mill so they picked someone they could spare. He let water fill the pipe without telling anyone. It was a miracle our dam did not burst. If it had, Kent and I would have been flushed down to the end of the dead-end pipe and caught in the strainer with no place to go, no air, and no way out.

Once the water pressure was removed, our dam worked fine again and we could complete the job. Kent and I installed two inches of concrete over the steel we had welded in place. Norm carried materials down to us. Kent and I mixed the mortar in buckets and trowel it on. The final step was to glue a plastic liner over the patch. We specified non-toxic glue and were assured the glue Engineering gave us was safe. Kent and I took the glue bucket down the pipe and start spreading it on the inside of the pipe. Engineering had given us contact cement. We got higher than a kite and after a bit sat back on burlap bags, laughing and admiring our work. Norm heard us—the pipe acted like a megaphone, sending our voices hundreds of feet up to the diving bell. He came hurtling down to drag us back to fresh air. We never did get the liner installed.

Example of a mill pipeline (steel with a concrete liner and a concrete casing) that Ken worked inside of.
California Coast (Date unknown) Devine collection.

Chapter 32: Crown Simpson

THE CROWN Simpson mill had the same basic design as the other mill, but with smaller effluent pipes. Like the other mill, the section of pipe running into the sea was made of steel encased in concrete. One pipe was three feet in diameter and the smaller pipe was two feet. In each case, the break in the pipe was in the surf, which is why Devine's was called in to fix it. The first job was to repair the larger pipe.

Before starting the repair, we had the mill put all the fluid through the pipe they could—the pressure of the fluid going through the break in the pipe dredged a giant hole in the sand, creating a space under the pipe for us to work in.

Kent Cochrane and I dove down and took a wide, stainless steel band with a flange on the edge and bolts to pull a foam liner tight around the pipe; this was a temporary fix that shut out the effluent escaping the pipe through the crack.

Next, Mick Leitz, Fred Devine's son-in-law and Devine's operations manager and later president, worked with the mill to design a huge dresser coupling hinged at the top with a wheel at each end, and a procedure to install it. The dresser coupling was a permanent solution that went around the outside of the pipe; it sealed against the pipe and was plumbed to pump grout between the coupling and the pipe.

The dresser coupling was heavy—we hired a helicopter to set it over the pipe. When hinged open, the dresser coupling looked like a giant butterfly. When the helicopter slacked off, the two halves of the coupling relaxed over the pipe. We jacked up the wheels so the dresser coupling was supported on the wheels, and used come alongs above and below the break to move the giant patch and center it over the stainless steel band Kent and I had installed. We let down the jacks and the dresser coupling relaxed over the pipe. The dresser coupling had a rubber seal and bolts to pull the seal tight. There were two stand pipes sticking out of the body of the dresser coupling for adding grout; the helicopter dragged out a three-inch grout hose for filling the void between the coupling and the pipe with concrete. It was a pretty routine job with no troubles.

We never had trouble with this mill.

Another time, the same mill had a two-foot pipe next to the main three-foot pipe used for emergencies if the main pipe went down. The offshore section of the small pipe had fallen into a gap caused by shifting sand, creating a two-foot, moon-shaped opening at the top of the pipe. At high tide the break was underwater and the surf filled the pipe with sand. For this job, an external dresser coupling wasn't going to do the job; we needed to seal the pipe from the inside. A two-foot diameter pipe isn't very big. Each day I crawled inside, dragging a flexible suction hose thru the pipe to suck out the sand. It was totally black. To repair the pipe, I had to design an internal dresser coupling, but this break caused the pipe to be offset, so a round coupling wouldn't work, plus the pieces of the internal coupling had to fit through an opening in the pipe located on the beach behind a sand dam. Once in place, the coupling had to expand and seal in one motion. I couldn't see the break so I had to feel everything and measure with my fingers, building the coupling in my head, taking into consideration the break and the offset. I'd be working in the pipe for hours and hours with a crew waiting at the other end of the sand dunes where I had entered the pipe.

The company had an engineer flown up from California. He knew what I was going through and told the others, "When Ken comes out, don't talk to him." He knew I couldn't be distracted before we got over to the engineering office and drew up what was in my head.

The coupling had to be in four parts. The two side connectors were the key to expand it. It was quite intricate the way it came together. When I tightened the bolts, the coupling expanded against the seals. This was the fun kind of job. The work had danger, but the people we worked with were competent so it was okay.

Chapter 33: First Arctic Dive

DURING THE period when the oil pipeline was being built across the interior of Alaska[21] we salvaged a couple of pipeline barges. The barges were identical in size—four hundred feet long, eighty feet wide and twenty-five feet deep—but different in configuration.

The Alaska pipeline is made up of four-foot-diameter, half-inch pipe in forty and sixty-foot sections.[22] The pipe sections were stacked on the barges and held in place with five- to six-foot-wide steel stanchions welded to the edge of the deck that tapered at the top. Cables across the load held the pipe in place.

The cables should have kept the load snug inside the stanchions, but, in heavy seas, the load sometimes shifted from side to side, eventually causing one or more stanchions to crack at the deck. The cracks let seawater into the hold, causing the barge to list to one side, making it easier for more seawater to enter the cracks. The heavy, reinforced deck of the barge made the vessel top heavy. These conditions combined to cause a couple of the barges to roll over.

Preparatory work started on the Alaska pipeline in 1969[23]. When Devine's got the call to salvage the first barge in September 1970, Mick Leitz and I flew up to Prudhoe Bay, the main base for oil companies drilling in the Arctic. We stayed at the Arco camp. One of their tugboats took us out to survey the job so we could determine what equipment we had to put together; the rest we would have to scavenge from the camp.

---

[21] In 1973 President Richard Nixon approved the construction of the Trans-Alaska Pipeline which was built and is managed by a consortium of seven oil companies holding exploration rights under the name Alyeska Pipeline Service. These companies include BP (47%), ConocoPhillips (28%), and Exxon Mobil (20%). Taking 3 years to complete, the 48-inch diameter pipeline was open for business in 1977. http://historical.whatitcosts.com/facts-alaska-pipeline.htm

[22] The pipeline is 800 miles long and fabricated from heavy wall cold weather steel pipe of 48" diameter in lengths of 40 and 60', imported from Japan. http://www.brighthubengineering.com/fluid-mechanics-hydraulics/84796-powering-the-alaska-pipeline/

[23] Total workforce (1969-1977): 70,000 http://tapseis.anl.gov/documents/docs/Section_13_May2.pdf

The Arctic Ocean was liquid only seven weeks of the year. The rest of the year it was frozen solid. When it's liquid it's full of icebergs. They break up. When the wind blows in one direction, there is open water. When it blows in the other direction, the open water closes up with pack ice. We had to hire two 5,000 horsepower tugs working twenty-four hours a day pushing ice to keep the water open at the work site.

It was September and we had only a few weeks to do the job. When we first got there, Mick and I stayed a night or two at the Arco camp. It was interesting. Modules had been brought in by barge, dragged across land, and put on pylons. You can't put equipment on tundra; it immediately starts to melt the ice and create a pool of water. If you put a bucket on the ground, in a few days there is a pool of water around the bucket. The Arco camp at Prudhoe Bay was elevated, built up on timbers above the permafrost. Heavy construction there is done in the winter when the ground is frozen solid.

The camp was an elaborate layout, like a huge hotel with wings radiating like a star and the entrance in the center. The camp had a recreation area with a huge restaurant at the back. To eat there, you got a tray and went past a row of counters where you could order anything you could think of and they would fix it for you. At the end of the row was a table full of all type of pies, cakes and cookies. Beside the table was a large bank of ice cream machines and freezers to make any kind of sundae. The restaurant was open twenty-four hours a day. Most of the guys working there gained weight; they'd go home and lose it, go back, and gain it again. With so little else to do or see, eating was a highpoint of the day. One wing of the complex was a greenhouse with tropical plants; the greenhouse helped clean the air and put new oxygen into it. Another wing had a movie theater with movies running all day and night. The rest of the wings were quarters for the guys living there working on the pipeline.

After the initial survey, Mick and I flew home, gathered up our gear, and flew back to Prudhoe Bay. Mick hired Eddie Forsythe from Commercial Divers to help us. We also hired a crane operator and deck hand from the pipeline. We hired a barge towing company out of Seattle with a base in Prudhoe to supply us with a personnel barge, a dive barge, and two tugs. The bigger personnel barge had a cook house and crane; the smaller dive barge was tied alongside the personnel barge. The dive barge had a bow ramp for rolling equipment to the beach. We put a forty-foot container on one end of the small barge for a dive shack—we could put on our dive gear, walk off the end of the bow ramp, and down we'd go. At night we slept in quarters on the tugs.

When we first arrived on the job, I was anxious to get into the water; I'd never been diving in the Arctic Ocean. I put on a custom-made wetsuit, jumped in, and went down to the bottom. I made all of my wetsuits using scissors and glue and neoprene, no nylon—a nylon surface makes a wetsuit easier to put on, but it's too cold; we used baby powder instead of nylon. With these suits we stayed relatively dry and had more mobility than with a dry suit. Each layer of the wetsuit was custom fit to the diver. The first layer was a 3/16" vest from neck to below the crotch and snug around armholes and neck. The 3/8" pants were custom fit to each diver and came up to just under the arms. A 3/8" pullover jacket went over the pants and had no zipper, the high neck went to just under the chin and high up the back of the neck to the head. The hood went over the flanges of the mask where it sealed against the face, with the mask strap on the outside, and had a slit for the mouth; the only pieces of skin exposed to the near-frozen seawater were our lips pursed thru the mouth slit and over the regulator mouthpiece, but they quickly went numb. A small bit of water could weep into the suit, but was warmed by our bodies as it slowly worked its way in. Our head would get wet when our hair wicked in seawater around the edges of the hood.

When I reached the bottom, I could see the bottom of the bay was odd, silty clay; not true clay or silt. If you picked up a handful and squashed it, it felt very rigid, but you could squeeze it. There was nothing else to see. No sand, no gravel, no nothing; just that odd, dark-grey clay. At the bottom, I found I was in a large groove, as if a giant plow had dug an eight-foot-deep furrow. As I swam along the furrow, I was wondering what caused it. I came to a place where another furrow crossed the one I was following. Then it dawned on me. The furrows were made by the bottoms of icebergs as they were blown across the ocean. Over the eons, icebergs had ground up the rock and made clay of it.

We anchored the work barges next to the capsized barge. The Arctic Ocean is very shallow here and when the barge rolled over, it dry docked itself on top of its load of pipe; we had a 400-foot barge with its hull out of the water, resting on top of its load.

Our first problem was to remove the load from under the barge. The large sections of pipe were held in place by a series of steel H-beam-like stanchions along each side of the barge and tied with chain straps. The other diver we hired, Eddie Forsythe, was tending me on deck. To get the barge back into the water, I swam under the edge of the barge and burned most of the way through each stanchion, leaving a little bit of steel to be burned through later. This weakened the stanchions and caused the load to push out, which made the barge want to come down.

Next, I burned the inside flanges, leaving a one-inch unburned section there, too. Away I went, burning the web of the H-flanges except for the one-inch sections I left as a keeper to hold each stanchion in position—I wanted the load to eventually push out the flanges, but stay in place until I was ready to burn off the one-inch keepers.

The barge was about four feet above me as I worked to burn through the keepers. I knew that at some point the remaining stanchions would break and the barge would come down on top of me. I wasn't worried. I knew the weakened stanchions would fly out, the pipe would roll out underneath me, and the barge would fall and simply shove me down into the water and there was nothing below to hurt me.

I don't remember which stanchion I was on, but I was going along burning my little one inch keepers when, all of a sudden, the rest of stanchions broke from the force of the cargo. Down came the barge. It looked pretty terrible from the diving rig. The guys knew I was underneath the barge, but I was okay. The pipe rolled out and we were able to secure the barge, which was floating upside down, the air trapped in the hull keeping it afloat.

Next Eddie and I plumbed the hatches with fittings to blow air into the various compartments to force out the water. To do this we removed the hatches underwater, took them to the surface where we welded on proper fittings, and dove to replace the hatches.

During all this, the two large tugs worked 24/7 to keep ice away from the site.

The next problem was that the barge was eighty feet wide, but where the barge rolled the water was only about fifty feet deep. We did not have enough room to parbuckle (rotate) the barge in the conventional fashion, which required that we place one edge of the barge on the bottom and pull the barge upright. We took the tugs and cruised around with a fathometer until we found a hole seventy-five feet deep. We towed the barge over to the hole and made up an anchoring system using anchors and chain we'd scavenged from the beach, the towing company, from other barges, and wherever else we could find them.

The anchoring system held the barge in place while we pulled against it with two ocean-going tugs to rotate it. I put three anchors in tandem on each of two anchor lines. Between each anchor we used heavy anchor chain. It was difficult to anchor in the clay bottom. We kept adding anchors until we could pull on them with the tugs without dragging the anchors. I was curious to see how the anchoring system worked in clay. I swam down the anchor chain to check it out. The chain had pulled through the clay and was settling into it. On the shoulder of each 3" diameter link of chain—for the entire length of the chain—was a mound of clay. At the end of the chain the anchors had rolled over and were not biting into the bottom. The links digging in the clay were the resistance, the anchors were just weights.

Finally, we flooded the barge, rotated it underwater, and pumped air in to displace the water and raise the barge to the surface where we could tow it back to Prudhoe Bay a few miles down the channel. After the barge was rolled, we patched a hole in the deck caused when one of the stanchions ripped.

To complete the salvage job we needed to pick up 300-some four-foot-wide, sixty-foot-long, half-inch thick steel pipe sections, load them onto lighter barges, and tow them into Prudhoe Bay. The specs on the pipe were stringent—there couldn't be any scratches. Eddie and I attached a nylon-lined steel glommer to each end of the pipe and the crane picked up each pipe section and set it on the barge. It took several days for Eddie and me to locate all the pipe sections. We kept count to be sure we had them all; we didn't want to leave any out there not only because of the salvage value, but, more importantly, we didn't want to leave anything in the shallow water to get tangled up with other barges coming into the bay. Some of the pipe had rolled quite a ways and we were missing one piece. I asked the guy keeping count if he was sure of the count. Yes. I stood on deck imagining the pipe. When the stanchions gave way, the pipe sections closest to the deck were out of the water and full of air; it would take time for water to rush in and make them sink. I was thinking the only direction the missing pipe could go was further than the sections we had already found, so I went out thirty or forty feet further from the outer reaches of our search area and there it was.

We heard later they rejected the whole load and used the pipe we salvaged for other purposes.

It took seventeen days to finish the job. Everything went well with no unexpected problems. It was the first major salvage job done in the Arctic Ocean, making it a one-of-a-kind experience.

The second pipeline barge we salvaged was unique in another way—the underwriter's rep wouldn't allow us to touch bottom. In the meantime, I had another one-of-a-kind experience diving in Alaska.

Chapter 34: Moonshine

NINETEEN-SEVENTY-FIVE was an interesting year in many ways. It was the year I quit Devine's, drank prohibition moonshine, got a bear hug from a Mexican frogman, lost one wife, but gained a new one and two more sons.

The spring of 1975 a chip barge sank just across the channel from Ketchikan, Alaska and Devine's got the salvage contract. I took one of the Devine crew, Larry, to tender for me and went up to meet with the underwriter's representative. I'd worked with this guy off and on for a couple of years. I told him we'd have to hire some local divers. He gave me the contact information for Alaska Diving Services; Dell Hanson was the owner.

Before we started work, the underwriter's rep gave me a little lecture, "Ken, we don't want any overtime on this job."

I said, "It's a salvage job. If we get doing something to roll the barge over, sometimes you get stuck, and you just have to work twenty-four hours a day to get the job done."

"I'm aware of all that," he said. "This is a small job in protected waters. I don't want any overtime on this job."

It was Ketchikan in the spring. It was a simple, safe, fun job in clear water. We would be working eight hours in days with sixteen hours of sunshine. *I don't know,* I wondered to myself, *Maybe this is his way of giving us a good job? Even with overtime, we can probably finish the job faster and for less cost if we keep on the job and get it done.*

I didn't understand the request, but said, "Fine."

I hired Dell and we proceeded to salvage the chip barge. It was a half-hour run by skiff across the bay. Each day we left the dock at 8:00 a.m. and about 4:30 p.m. we picked up our gear and returned to the dock; we got paid from the time we left the dock to the time we got back. Many, many times we were right in the middle of something and we'd have to shut everything down to avoid working overtime.

It was a very simple job. We had to patch a hole in the barge, roll it over right side up, and refloat it. Not rocket science, but there are certain things you have to do. We couldn't work weekends because that was overtime, so we were working forty hours a week and it made the job long, but there were highlights that made it worthwhile.

Dell was down working on a patch on the barge and had to wait for some parts. He was using a small helmet with a communication system. He called and told his tender, "I'm gonna drop to the bottom to look around while you get the part."

After a few minutes, Dell called back and said, "Have ya got that part for me?"

"Yeah."

"Wait. I'm gonna come up, but it's gonna be a little different. I'm right underneath the edge of the boat." He was in about forty feet of clear water. "Get ready. I'm gonna blow my suit up and float right up beside the boat. Get down on your hands and knees and get ready to grab me."

I wondered, *What's going on?*

The tender and I got on our hands and knees and pretty soon, there came Dell. Through the water we could see he had something on his belly and had his arms wrapped around whatever it was. The air in his dry suit was expanding as he rose and he looked like a big red bubble—he hit the surface flat out. That was when we could see he had a dozen bottles stacked on his stomach. We started removing them and saw some bottles had air bubbles in the glass, as old bottles do. The bottles were corked and crusted with barnacles.

Prohibition rum runners used to come up to Alaska from Canada. They put a dozen bottles to a burlap bag with the top tied. When the revenuers chased them, the rum runners would run a course next to shore in shallow water and throw the gunny sacks of bottles overboard in a line. Later, they would try to retrieve the bags with grapple hooks. They must have missed one, because Dell found these bottles still stacked in a pile, the burlap bag long gone.

At the end of our shift we placed the bottles in the skiff. Dell radioed a friend that was a bottle collector and he agreed to meet us at the dock in Ketchikan.

On the way across the Bay, we were looking at the bottles.

"This stuff must be well aged," one of the guys said.

Someone else suggested, "Let's pop a cork and see if it's any good."

We opened a bottle and took a drink. It was raspy, but drinkable. Turns out whiskey stops aging when it's bottled; it doesn't work like wine. Plus, this was moonshine out of someone's still and had never seen a wood cask. We passed the bottle around to the divers, tenders, and the crane operator. Not bad! It was a couple of miles across the bay to Ketchikan. We arrived at the dock half lit.

Dell's friend, the bottle collector, was waiting for us. He made nice comments on our find and added, "These are good collector bottles."

They were old, pretty bottles crusted with marine growth. Dell asked the collector what he thought they were worth, and he answered, "Well, a minimum of $1,500 apiece....full," he said and looked over at the one we had uncorked and drank. Good thing the bay wasn't any farther across—we would have had time to uncork another one!

After the job was complete, Dell, my tender Larry, and I decided to take a float plane to a lake with a cabin and trout fish. Not a bad little job. Dell and I are still friends; he's a good guy. Later I hired him for a dive in Mexico.

This was the job I wanted my son Eric to come on. It only cost $96 for a plane ticket, and it would have been so much fun for him, but he was eleven at the time, and his mom wouldn't let him go. Sandy and I were still together, but, as I found out, that was about to change.

Chapter 35: Don't Touch Bottom

THE DAY AFTER I got home after finishing the Ketchikan job I got a call for another job with Devine's to rescue another pipe barge in Alaska. This barge was similar to the pipe barge we salvaged five years earlier in Prudhoe Bay—it came from Japan with a load of four-foot-diameter half-inch steel pipe. This one capsized in the Aleutian Islands so off I went to the western-most edge of the United States.

The pipe sections were loaded like logs on the deck between five-foot wide stanchions that narrowed at the top. To save money during construction, the stanchions were welded to the deck, not integrated into the hull structure, which was fine for calm seas, but not the harsh conditions in the Arctic. In heavy seas, the load shifted—the pressure against the stanchions created cracks in the deck and eventually opened the deck like a can opener. The seas washing over the deck filled in through the cracks, the incoming water went to the lowest point (as designed), but in heavy seas the lowest point wasn't the bottom of the vessel and the seawater in the hull stayed a little to one side, making the barge list, making it easier for more seawater to enter the cracks. As more water came in, the list increased, and the top-heavy barge eventually turned over.

The capsized vessel was a brand-new 400-foot-long barge, 80 feet wide, and 25 feet deep. It had longitudinal bulkheads, not transverse like most vessels. The rake tanks at each end—used for flotation—were transverse. The longitudinal bulkheads were set 25 feet on each side, with a larger 30-foot compartment in the center.

The odd thing was the bulkheads on this barge were spot welded, not sealed. The theory was that incoming water would settle in the bottom, keeping the vessel upright, but what happened is, due to the sea swell causing the barge to list a bit to one side, the incoming water went to one side and stayed there. When the barge rolled in heavy seas and the heavy pipe load shifted, it opened holes in the deck on one side, which allowed seawater to flood in and flip it over. The chains across the top of the pipe broke and, this time, the load sank. Like the previous pipe barge, the reinforced deck made the barge top heavy and, once the barge flipped, it trapped air in the solid hull and the vessel floated upside down.

The *Sudbury*

The *Sudbury*, an old ex-salvage tug operated by the Canadian company Seaspan, towed the flipped barge to Amchitka Island, near the end of the Aleutian chain. Amchitka was the site of the largest nuclear test in the United States and had been a big airport during World War II.[24] A number of U.S. military vessels were sunk there when the Japanese attacked and invaded the island during the war. Those vessels are still there. While diving I picked up live ammunition and other artifacts from the seafloor.

At the time we were there, the huge airport, buildings, and natural harbor were deserted. We charted an airliner to take us and our equipment out to the empty base. It was cold and foggy. The plane dumped Doc Stream, the surveyor, me, and our gear on the tarmac. Doc had a radio. The *Sudbury* heard us come in. The crew broke into one of the hangars and hotwired an abandoned Atomic Energy Commission truck to pick us up.

The *Sudbury* was about two hundred feet long. It was a little short of salvage equipment, and the gear it did have was antiquated with old-style multi-shiv blocks instead of winches, and an inadequate anchoring system, but it made a good work platform. Whenever we needed equipment for the project, I'd tell the crew of the *Sudbury* what we needed and they would scrounge the base for it.

The barge was floating upside down, the stern lower than the bow, which was elevated by the air trapped in the forward rake tank; only the rake tank bulkheads had full welds and were sealed for flotation. We needed to seal the other

---

[24] Amchitka (Aleut: Amchixtax) is a volcanic, tectonically unstable island in the Rat Islands group of the Aleutian Islands in southwest Alaska. It is part of the Alaska Maritime National Wildlife Refuge. The island is about 68 kilometers (42 mi) long, and from 3 to 6 km (1.9 to 3.7 mi) wide. The area has a maritime climate, with many storms, and mostly overcast skies... Amchitka was selected by the United States Atomic Energy Commission to be the site for underground detonations of nuclear weapons. Three such tests were carried out: Long Shot, an 80-kiloton (330 TJ) blast in 1965; Milrow, a 1-megaton (4.2 PJ) blast in 1969; and Cannikin in 1971 – at 5 Mt (21 PJ), the largest underground test ever conducted by the United States. The tests were highly controversial, with environmental groups fearing that the Cannikin explosion, in particular, would cause severe earthquakes and tsunamis. Amchitka is no longer used for nuclear testing. It is still monitored for the leakage of radioactive materials. http://en.wikipedia.org/wiki/Amchitka

compartments so we flew three welders up from the States. One of the welders had never been diving, but had to in order to get under the barge and inside for welding. We got him suited up and I took him by the hand and said, "Don't do anything but breathe normally. I'll take you in."

He was a bit nervous, but said he knew what he was in for before he volunteered for the job. He went into the clear, frigid water and I followed. We entered the hull by swimming in through the rips in the deck from the torn stanchions. After that, he had no trouble suiting up like the rest of the guys and going into the hull on his own.

We pumped in air to dry the compartment the welders would be working in. To make the compartments airtight, the welders had to close the gaps between the original spot welds—350 feet on each side plus 25 feet for each of the six bulkheads—850 feet in all. It took the three welders a month of working from extension ladders in a cold hull illuminated with string lights to seal the compartments. We had to constantly pump in fresh air to flush out the welder smoke. Smoke burbled out the rips in the deck.

Day after day of welding and, finally, we got the compartments on one side of the barge sealed and isolated from the side with the torn stanchions. We put plumbing in the compartment hatches and then had to find some rigging so we could par buckle (rotate) the barge. The plumbing allowed us to remove water and add air or vice versa as needed to in order to get the barge to rotate the way we wanted it to.

The barge was in about seventy-five feet of water off one of the piers left over from the war. I knew I had to sink the vessel on its side to pull it over and upset the differential between the deck weight and the bottom weight. In order to accommodate large loads, the deck weight of a barge is considerably heavier than the hull; it wants to float upside down by nature. The deck weight had to be offset by pulling the barge past center to get it to roll. I counted on the sea bottom being slightly sloped; when the edge of the hull touched the bottom, the barge would be perpendicular and by pulling on it with the *Sudbury's* old-style blocks and multi-shivs we could roll it over. We scrounged up an anchoring system to hold the Sudbury in place and started to pump air into the barge. To get the deck to come up right, the air bubble had to go against the deck, not the bottom. As it turned out, my biggest problem in getting the vessel right side up wasn't with the *Sudbury's* old equipment.

Vessels and cargoes are usually insured by several underwriters. The underwriters do not do the actual salvage—they hire someone to act as their representative. For this job, the underwriters hired Doc Stream of U.S. Salvage to be their joint representative. Doc's role was to observe what was going on during the salvage and report back to the insurance companies. In some cases, the representative has the authority to hire the salvage company. Doc was a very nice, elderly gentleman with whom I'd done many previous jobs.

This time Doc told me, "Ken, whatever you do, you can't touch this barge down on the bottom."

I couldn't understand why. He had no authority and no knowledge of what was needed for this salvage job. Maybe he didn't want to get a dent in the hull? But the barge's top was already opened up like a can, and a little dent in the hull wasn't going to hurt it. Anyway, he gave me a good lecture about it. He did not want that barge to touch bottom. I knew I couldn't salvage the barge without touching bottom because at the angle the barge would go down as we pumped air into it, the low point had to touch bottom to offset some of the weight of the heavy deck; the *Sudbury* did not have enough horsepower to offset the weight by itself.

I calculated the tide, which only varied two to four feet, to find the point of touch needed to offset the weight of the deck and started the pumps. It took twenty-four hours to pump out seawater and add air to the sealed compartments. In the process, the barge started to roll. At one point Doc came stomping into the wheelhouse, "Ken, I'm almost sure it's touching bottom!"

I didn't want to lie to him, so I said, "Doc, don't worry about it. I'm taking care of it."

If I miscalculated, I could sink the barge and pump it full of air to bring it up right side up. I went to bed in the middle of the night, the pumps still running. It was only a matter of finishing the dewatering. I hadn't been to bed for I don't know how long. By morning, most of the deck was out of the water and the barge came right side up. In the process the side of the barge touched bottom, but you couldn't tell from looking at it.

I was picking up gear getting ready to come home when Mick Leitz's sister-in-law and Devine's receptionist, Marilyn, called on the single side band radio. The reception was pretty squawky.

"When are you going to be done, Ken?" Marilyn asked. "You've got to be home immediately. Mick took the *Salvage Chief* to Mexico and he's in trouble. You've got to come home quick."

The oil pipeline company flew an airliner all the way out to Amchitka to pick up me, Doc Stream, and the extra crew we brought in to help. The tug crew finished the job by picking up the anchors, securing the barge, and towing it home.

I think Doc Stream retired not too long after that project and I didn't work with him again so I never did find out why he didn't want me to touch bottom.

Chapter 36: Best Diver World

WHILE PART of the Devine crew, including myself, was pumping out the Japanese pipe barge in the Aleutians, Mick and the rest of the company had gone to Mexico with the *Salvage Chief* to salvage a sunken dredge and they were having problems. I flew home from Alaska and a day later was on my way to Mexico.

The dredge was sunk inside the mouth of two jetties where a jungle river exited into the ocean. Puerto Madero is about fourteen miles north of the Guatemala border. In 1975 it was just a village on a jungle river. Today it is a holiday resort and surfing destination.

The *Dredge Oregon*, sister to the dredge that sank in Mexico.

The Mexican government had purchased a large pipeline dredge from a company in Texas to dredge the harbor. This dredge was a sister ship to the *Dredge Oregon*.[25] The deal required the Texas company to tow the dredge inside the jetties at Puerto Madero and drop the spuds. The vessel was 67 feet long and 20 feet wide with a 5.5-foot draft. Each spud was 104 feet long and weighed 34 tons. Besides holding the dredge in place, the spuds could be raised and lowered to act as pivot points for the dredge to swing it one way or the other. Once the dredge was secured on the spuds, the Texas company got paid and went home.

The trouble here was the jetties were not fully extended—when a storm came out of the west, the swell built up in the shallow water inside the mouth of the jetties. The dredge was riding the high surf, up and down, up and down, on the spuds. When the tide went out, the jerking caused the cables that set the spuds to come tight and ripped the stern winch off at the deck, opening a hole in the deck.

---

[25] http://freeassociationdesign.wordpress.com/2012/07/20/columbia-migrations-dredge-oregon/
http://www.waheagle.com/news/article.exm/2009-10-
01_on_the_oregon__keep_the_channel_clear

Dredges are very shallow vessels, with the deck close to the water. Once the deck had a hole in it, waves washing over the deck promptly sank the dredge.

The Mexican government originally hired a company from Los Angeles, a company I'd never heard of, to start the salvage operation. From time to time, they put in for pay draws, but literally did nothing. It was all phony.

When Mick heard the Mexicans were looking for someone to salvage the dredge, he got in touch with them. They were a bit upset about the previous operation, so Mick made them a deal. The vessel was beyond economic repair. We would do a harbor clearance job, not a salvage job. Devine's were not trying to salvage the vessel, just trying to clear the harbor entrance by taking the dredge around the end of the jetties and sink it in deeper water so the Mexicans could deepen the channel with another dredge.

When I got there, Mick and his crew had been in Mexico about a month. The dredge sank right side up. The plan was to roll the dredge upside down and use the bottom, which was sealed, to trap air underneath to lighten the dredge enough to float one end and tow it offshore. However, the vessel was angled in a way that did not make it practical to roll.

The backup plan was to seal the decks airtight so we could blow in air while it was upright, then raise one end, and drag it offshore. The problem with this idea is the decks were thin and the house that had been on top of the deck had been ripped off by storms—the deck was practically shredded. One crack was around fourteen feet long. Mick originally bid the job on a flat fee and ended up going back to the Mexican government to renegotiate the price to cover the added cost of patching the deck.

One of the rules for working in Mexico required us to use local equipment—if you needed a pump, and if any Mexican manufacturer made a pump, you had to buy a Mexican pump. This rule didn't affect us too much because we had our own pumps on the *Salvage Chief.*

In the three months I was there, we put fifty-four major patches on the deck. Once again, Kent Cochran and I were a team. Kent was a little younger and shorter than me (I'm about 5'11") and the father of two little boys. He was a good welder and mechanic; he was a hard worker and never gave anyone any trouble.

Kent and I did all the patching. The patches were bolted on with rubber seals so the air would stay inside when the hull was inflated. Kent worked the inside of the vessel and I worked outside. Loose pieces of steel from the destroyed house were moving about in the surf. Once, when I felt a particularly big surge coming, I hung on to something, then heard a bunch of clattering. It was too murky to see clearly. I reached out to finish my job and there was a big sheet of steel laying there. It could have cut me in half.

To make the project even more difficult, the hull was full of sand and palm leaves that had come down the river and drifted in through the holes in the deck. We built an airlift and poked it through the deck for the divers to suck out the debris and lighten the vessel enough to move it. At the same time, we were patching the deck. We'd patch a compartment and test it by blowing air into it, to make sure it was airtight, then move on to the next compartment.

We were making progress, but because of being burned by the first operation, the Mexicans were a little nervous. We had been on the job for six or eight weeks, but, from the beach, it looked like nothing was happening—the *Salvage Chief* was just sitting there day after day with no visible sign of progress. Midway through the project, the Mexican government sent three or four of their Armada (Navy) frogmen to inspect our work.

Summer in Mexico is hurricane season. We were working in the surf where the sea meets a muddy jungle river and it was often stormy. The water was black and turbulent; it was no place for an inexperienced diver and I wasn't sure how much experience these Mexican frogmen had. I got an idea. We had a Mexican representative on site. Ricardo was in charge of West Coast marine operations and spoke English; he acted as our go-between with the locals and the Mexican officials.

I told Ricardo, "Go ahead and get them out here."

When they arrived, I told Ricardo to tell the frogmen I would take each one of them down to the vessel, one at a time. The frogman could do an inspection, then I'd bring him out and repeat the process with each of the others.

"Okay," I said. "Here's how we're going to do it. I'm going to tie a line to your wrist." I showed the Mexican divers a six-foot piece of cord. "And the first thing we have to do is get inside the vessel, which is a little tricky. We have to go through a hatch and there is surf rolling over the vessel."

As the surf rolled over the dredge it pushed water in, and as it passed by it sucked water out. It was like a giant toilet flushing the water up and down, up and down through the openings in the wreck. I took each frogman down to the wreck and I went through the hatch on the right "flush." When I could feel the water moving in the right direction, I'd pull the line and whoosh, in came the Mexican diver.

The water was black and the only light came from my headlamp. I took each of the Mexican divers through the compartments and over to where ours divers were working sucking up sand and debris with the air lifts. I'd shine the light on our diver, point, and then move on to the next compartment. Of course, the frogmen were instantly lost in the darkness.

I showed them the patches we'd put on the deck. I did this three times, once with each Mexican diver. When I got the third diver out, they started jabbering amongst themselves in Spanish. Of course, I couldn't understand a word. They were relating their individual experiences, which had scared each of them to death. After a bit, the lead diver came over, put a big hug on me, and said in broken English, "Best diver world!"

We all had a laugh about that. Best diver world. That was a high point.

During the operation, several of our thirty crew members got very sick with extremely high fevers. The river was flushing raw sewage from the Chiapas state capital of Tapachula, and we were diving in it. Ironically, the divers did not get sick. The deckhands and tenders, the guys on deck handling lines and taking care of the divers, caught the fever. The *Salvage Chief's* first mate, Bob Bracken, an old Coast Guard Commander, had some medical training. He pumped the sick tenders and deckhands full of antibiotics and put them in their bunks.

The air temperature was around 110 degrees Fahrenheit every day and the humidity was high. The *Salvage Chief's* deck and hull were painted black and there was no air conditioning. It was brutal inside the ship. The only way to sleep was nude on a sheet with an oscillating fan for each bunk running up and down your body. As long as the fan ran and you had no clothes on, you could sleep. If the fan went off, it was unbearable.

After about a week, the guys who were sick recovered. We never knew what they had.

The illnesses delayed the project and we were running out of food. We told Ricardo we needed some meat. He arranged some beef to be delivered the following week. The next week, a pickup truck pulled up to the pier and parked on the jetty. Two guys jumped out of the truck and walked out onto the pier toting large black plastic garbage bags. We took the skiff over and down came the meat. They had butchered a Brahma bull. They did not have a refrigeration system so the meat was very fresh. It was boned and cut lengthwise, just bags and bags of strips of raw meat. The cook did the best he could with it. We ate a lot of Brahma bull and potatoes.

Like I said, it was the summer storm season. Every once in a while a big hurricane would come in. When a large storm hit, we'd go into town to spend several days and take a break. One day, we were diving when a storm came up sooner than expected. By the time we got out of the water, the swell was really rolling. The *Salvage Chief* was anchored off what was to be the new channel entrance. The seas were huge and we couldn't launch the skiff so we were stuck on board. The skipper had gone to town earlier to see his wife. The second in charge, Bob, was in charge of the *Salvage Chief*, but not the divers; he didn't have authority to keep us on board.

I told my diving partner Kent, "I'm not going to lay out here for four or five days. We're going to the hotel where it's comfortable."

He asked, "How are we going to get off the ship?"

I told him, "Get your town clothes, put them in a garbage bag, tie the end, and then tie it again. Make up two bags. We'll put on our wetsuits and fins."

He got his bags and followed me to the fantail at the rear of the ship. The *Chief* was in the surf facing seaward. When a big swell came under the ship, I felt the deck come up, and knew the swell would carry us away from the ship. I shouted, "Jump!"

Away we went. We caught the swell and with the bags for flotation and our fins pumping, we surfed all the way to the beach. Mick was in a truck on shore and picked us up. The rest of the guys had to stay on board.

Devine's had a large crew on this job. Besides the *Chief's* crew of about twenty, there were seven divers. Allen, a beginning diver served as tender; Dell Hanson, who found the moonshine on the bottom of the bay by Ketchikan and whom I had come down from Alaska Diving Services to help us; the second engineer's son, who'd been a diver in the Gulf of Mexico; Kent Cochrane and I.

Mick also hired two divers from the original L.A. operation. We called them the Beach Bums. I finally had to take them out of the water; they were dangerous. This pissed them off. One had to leave to go into the National Guard Reserve so he wasn't a problem, but the second Beach Bum still had issues with my decision. I could see they were nervous and uncomfortable in the water. That made them dangerous to themselves and other divers. You can't be that way when you are a professional.

One day when we were in town the second Beach Bum came to my hotel room and confronted me.

"Why did you take me out of the water?" he asked.

"You're dangerous," I told him. "You don't belong there. You're not comfortable."

"How do you know that?" he demanded.

The divers wore helmets and had communication with their tenders on deck. Generally, this diver and Dell worked together clearing the debris out of the same section of the wreck. Dell was on one suction and the Beach Bum was on the other suction. When Dell talked to his tender, he stopped siphoning the sand out. I had often seen the discharge end—it came clean when Dell talked to his tender. That meant the other diver was not pumping sand either. He was always talking to his tender; that told me he was nervous. A diver can't talk to his tender and work at the same time. It was black in there and he had to feel the work with his hands; you have to think about what you are doing and can't be talking at the same time as you are working.

Plus, we had bailout bottles, a small reserve bottle of air with a regulator that went into the primary system to be used in case of emergency. If his main air hose got stuck, the diver could reach down and turn the valve, which allowed him to breathe normally for ten or fifteen minutes giving him time to get out of the water.

"Every day you come out of the vessel, you have to go pump your reserve bottle up. That means you're testing it. It means you're nervous."

When I told him how I identified the problem, he agreed with me.

I told him, "When we have diving jobs that I feel you're safe on, I'll put you back in."

He agreed. After that we became pretty good friends.

By fall (1975), we were still working the Mexican dredge project. Allen, Kent, and I had been home three days since spring and we decided to have our wives come down. We called them and said, "Get a flight down here in two days. The six of us are going to go on a big Mexican vacation."

Bob, the mate, knew we spent time off the ship. Kent and I had a hotel room in town where we could escape the heat of the ship. It was too hot to stay on board all the time. There were girls everywhere desperate to make some money. I met one and found out her circumstances. We didn't speak the same language, but it was easy to see the situation.

Bob had these packets of pills. It was a one shot deal. We didn't know if we had anything, but if we took a packet and gave the wives a packet to take, they'd be protected. Bob knew all the wives. He made up a packet for each one and added a personal note. Sandy's note said, "Sandy, these pills will help protect you from jungle diseases, Bob."

The day came and the plane landed at the airport. My wife and I were childhood sweethearts; I knew her very, very well. Sandy was the last one off the plane. As she came down the airplane steps, I looked at her. Kent was standing next to me. I turned to him and said, "Kent, something's wrong. I've got to prepare myself for the worst."

We gave the girls the pills and rushed them back to the hotel. I sat Sandy down and said, "Sandy, we've known each other a long time. We may as well put it on the table and deal with it, whatever it is."

She told me she'd been seeing Dean, my friend from the Sheriff's River Patrol. "I want a divorce," she said, "but we can still have our Mexican vacation."

"You mean you've been expressing your love for Dean and you still want a Mexico vacation with me?" I asked her. "No. We're going to go home and welcome Dean into the family."

We agreed it was divorce time. Sandy and I flew home the next day, no Mexican vacation.

On the way back to Portland we had a layover in Mexico City. We got a room with two beds. Over a very nice dinner we talked and talked about the kids. When we went back to the room, I ask Sandy, "Which bed do you want? I want to lay out my clothes and take a shower."

"You don't have to sleep alone," she said.

We had a nice going away party.

Chapter 37: Quitting Devine's

AFTER COMING home from Mexico from salvaging the dredge, I was thinking about the time I pictured the tunnel that represented my life. I decided I'd done everything I could do at Devine's. I had had all those experiences. During the period from 1965 to 1975 we had had many successes. We took on every job that came our way. We never failed and we never seriously hurt anybody. It may not appear in a history book, but those of us who were there knew it was a record that could never be equaled. The company was rolling.

I went to Mick Leitz, who had taken over as president after Fred Devine retired, and told him I was going to quit. He didn't believe me. It took me a month to quit. Mick kept calling me for jobs, but I didn't take them. Finally, I had a meeting with him and the accountant. Mick offered to sell me part of the company, cheap.

"No. I'm done here," I told him.

"What are you going to do?" he asked.

"I don't know, but it's going to be different."

It was time to go. I loved working for Fred Devine Diving and Salvage Company. As long as there was a challenge, it was enjoyable. Devine's was at the top of the salvage game again, but I knew it was time for me to do something else. I was never a regular employee; I and the other divers had kept our independence. That changed after I left.

When I first went to work for Devine's, Fred Devine couldn't afford a lot of fulltime divers so we were on an on-call basis and went on the payroll only for the duration of each job. If we wanted to, we could turn down jobs. When Mick finally realized I was serious about quitting, he called a meeting of the tenders and on-call divers, including Kent and Allen, who had been with me on the Mexico job, and told them, "We're not going to have any more Ken Dyes in this company. You're either going to go on the payroll fulltime or you're outta here."

About three days later, Kent came over to where I was working at Sportcraft. He thought Mick's meeting was funny and came to tell me about it. It was a joke;

Mick was just upset. The guys were glad to go on salary. Later, Kent and another diver left Devine's to form Advanced American Diving.

Chapter 38: Devine Postscript

(What happened to Devine's after you left? Ken laughed and said,)

ACTUALLY, THEY started making even more money. A year after I left, a super tanker tied to the dock in San Pedro, California, inside the bay, blew up. Mick called me and asked me to come by the office. When I arrived, he said, "I just got back from San Pedro and had an interesting experience I want to share with you."

He told me about the fire, people killed, and how the ship sank in the bay. It would be a huge job to cut up and remove the wreckage. The Insurance companies sent out invitations to bid and held a pre-bid conference. They invited Mick. The meeting was in a big hall; Mick was a little late. He walked in to see big tables and 40 to 50 people sitting around.

"Mr. Leitz," one of the men at the main table greeted him, "we're glad to see you could make it. Come up here, we want you to sit here at the head of the table."

The meeting had been going on before Mick got there, but he had no warning of how it was going to go.

The head guy turned to Mick and said, "Mr. Leitz, we've heard about your company. Would you like to take this project on at a cost-plus basis, plus 15%?"

It wasn't a pre-bid conference at all— Fred Devine Diving and Salvage Company was the only bidder.

They made a ton of money. There weren't enough divers available trained to burn steel so Devine's set up a diving school at the site. After removing the steel, there was all that oil to clean up. Mick designed and built a device to float across the bay to suck up the oil that settled in the low spots and separate it from the seawater.

Mick just wanted to share the story with me; he knew I was on to other things.

I got out at the right time. The salvage business has changed. For example, the *Salvage Chief* was onsite and ready to pull off the *New Carissa*[26] the day it went aground on the Oregon coast in February 1999, but the US Coast Guard would not allow them to do it; they must have figured the big tug coming up from California could tow it off better than the *Chief* could winch it off, but the same weather that caused the *New Carissa* to go aground in the first place kept pushing her further and further into the sand and she broke in half before the tug could get to her.

In the old days, the Coast Guard was a good outfit that took people off grounded boats and did what they could to secure the site. When the salvage crew showed up, the Coast Guard took off and the salvage operators took over. I don't know what happened that now allows them to take on more than they can handle.

A year or two after the *New Carissa* went aground, an old wood tug sank at one of my moorages. The mooring lines were pointing straight down and you couldn't see the boat. Diesel was bubbling up from the fuel tank vent pipes so I jumped in and sealed them off and arranged for a crane to lift the boat up. By law, we contacted the Coast Guard. I'd just gotten out of the water from plugging the fuel vents when a young Coast Guard guy came up to the dock with a clipboard in his hand. He asked me my name. I could tell he was feeling pretty important and was going to make sure the rules were enforced. He looked at his clipboard, then looked at me, and said I wasn't a qualified diver. I laughed.

A crowd of customers from the marina had formed on the dock. They were there to help, not just watch. One of the boaters put an oil containment boom in the water downstream of the site. As oil spots formed from the diesel fuel that burbled to the surface from the fuel vent, another boater tossed a bilge pad on the spot. A bilge pad or diaper looks like a large, thick paper towel; it soaks up oil, but not water, and it floats. The river current piled the now oily bilge diapers against the oil boom. When the diapers were four of five deep against the boom, the current pulled the bottom diapers under the boom and they drifted down stream. One of the marina customers got into his skiff and started to pick up the drifting oil-soaked

---

[26] The M/V New Carissa was a freighter that ran aground on a beach near Coos Bay, Oregon, United States, during a storm in February 1999 and subsequently broke apart. An attempt to tow the bow section of the ship out to sea failed when the tow line broke, and the bow was grounded again. Eventually, the bow was successfully towed out to sea and sunk. The stern section remained on the beach near Coos Bay. Fuel on board the ship was burned off *in situ*, but a significant amount was also spilled from the wreckage, causing ecological damage to the coastline. The United States Coast Guard performed an investigation and found that captain's error was the main cause of the wreck; however, no criminal liability was established and the captain and crew were not charged. There were significant legal and financial consequences for the ship's owners and insurer. The stern section remained aground for over nine years. It was dismantled and removed from the beach in 2008. http://en.wikipedia.org/wiki/New_Carissa

diapers and put them into a plastic garbage bag. The Coast Guard told him he wasn't qualified to handle hazardous waste and ordered him to stop. He sat back, folded his arms, looked directly at the Coast Guard guy, and asked evenly, "What do you want me to do?"

The oil-soaked diapers were making their way to the yacht club next door.

"OK," the Coast Guard relented. "I guess you can pick them up."

We had a large crane come in to lift the tug. The pumps weren't making any headway; there was a fist-sized hole below the water line that was refilling the boat. I saw a tennis ball floating nearby and told Eric, "Grab that tennis ball and plug the hole in the tug."

The Coast Guard guy saw Eric go in the water and yelled, "You can't do that! You've got to be suited up."

It didn't make any more sense than anything else he'd said and the tennis ball did the job—the pumps got out enough water for the crane to lift the tug.

My own actions to keep diesel fuel out of the river got me written up as 'non-cooperative.' It's a shame when rules are more important than results and when the people in charge are not responsible for results.

Chapter 39: Lloyd's of London Offer

WHILE I WAS still working for Devine's, all the major marine industries in the area received an invitation from Lloyd's of London Salvage to attend a dinner with the secretary of Lloyd's who was going to be visiting Portland. The secretary is similar to a company president here. There was a local Lloyd's rep we all worked with who did the invitations. He invited Mick Leitz, the president, and Captain Mattila from Devine's, and specifically asked that I be there.

Riedel International was also invited. Arthur Riedel, Sr. was a hell of a man. He built Willamette Western, a big marine construction company. His son, Art Jr., went to the best colleges. We nicknamed him "Artie-baby." Artie-baby was invited to the meeting, too. He and I had a problem and had had several confrontations over the years and there was always tension between us.

There was a reception with cocktails before dinner. We were in this big hall having cocktails when the local Lloyd's of London rep came in and announced, "The Secretary is here and wants to meet each of you. Please line up and I'll take him by to meet you."

Art Jr. was standing on one side of me and Captain Mattila and Mick were on the other side. The Secretary came down the line and was introduced to Art. "Glad to meet you," he says, blah, blah, blah.

"And this is Ken Dye of..."

"Ken Dye! I've wanted to meet you for a long time," the Secretary exclaimed. "You need to sit by me at dinner. We have a lot to talk about."

The secretary and I sat together and talked salvage all through dinner. I want to keep ego out of this book, but that was a pretty heady experience. I found out later he was sizing me up to go to the East Coast.

When I quite Devine's, I was out of work. Lloyd's knew about it and wanted to sponsor me to set up a marine salvage operation on the East Coast.

"The East Coast has seven times more shipping than the West Coast," the Lloyd's rep explained. "Therefore, we have seven times more wrecks. The salvage companies there don't have the same expertise as you do. We want you to move to the East Coast and we'll connect you with the right people."

I was at a turning point in my life. I had fulfilled the voice's prophesy of becoming a professional diver. The block in the tunnel I had seen six years ago told me that my career as a salvage diver was going to come to an end. This seemed to me to be that end—I had come to the block in the tunnel.

It was flattering to be approached in that way by Lloyd's, but I didn't want to start a business on the East Coast. There was no place for me to go here, I just knew I wasn't supposed to go there. I had Sportcraft Landing, the moorage in Oregon City, to work on, but other than that I didn't know what I was going to do.

Several changes had taken place in my life in a short time: I left Devine's and got divorced within a couple of weeks of each other. Within two weeks of that I met my future wife.

When you look at the whole picture—starting with Croft & Neville, and all the near misses that never seriously hurt anyone, and all the successes I had in spite of difficult circumstance—it is clear there was a spiritual presence guiding me. I waited to see what would come next.

Part 5: Time for a Change

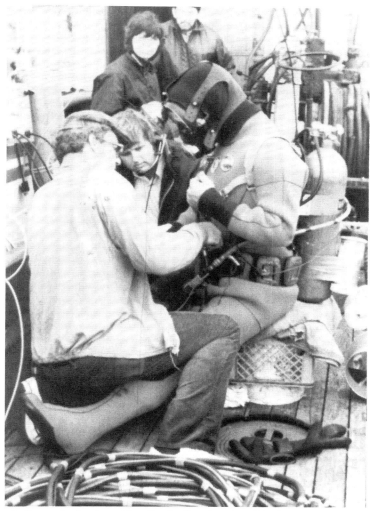

Suiting up to dive for gold on the *Brother Jonathan* (1977)
From Left to Right: Dick Long, Connie Schweiger, Kathy Dye, a guy from
Eureka (standing in background), and Ken Dye in dry suit.
(Dick is sitting on Ken's leg, which is in a full cast inside of the dry suit)

Chapter 40: Kathy

AFTER LEAVING Devine's, I had a major change ahead of me. I knew I was still going to dive, but I didn't know how, why, when, or where. Sportcraft Landing was doing well. Except for the divorce from Sandy, I was pretty happy.

Larry was a dive tender I helped get into Devine's; we worked together on the mill pipeline in California where Kent and I were almost flushed out to sea, in Alaska when Dell found the moonshine bottles, and other jobs. Larry was a single guy who kidded me about finding me a woman. Of course, I was married all those years and not interested, but he liked to tease me about girlfriends. It had been a big joke. After the divorce, I went to Larry and said, jokingly, "Well, I'm divorced now. How about all those women you're always talking about? You got any you can fix me up with?"

"I don't really know any you'd be interested in," he confessed.

A couple of weeks later, Larry called me. He was all excited and said, "Ken, I've found you a woman."

I said, "What are you talking about?"

He was dating a nurse at the time. He said, "My girlfriend has a friend and we helped her move this weekend from Bend to Tualatin. She works in the OR (operating room) at the hospital. I think you'd really like this gal."

I told him to go ahead and set it up. I was 35 years old and Kathy was 29 with two little boys.

Kathy Dye (1977)

Larry tried to get Kathy to go out with me, but she didn't know me and was uncomfortable with the idea of a blind date, but felt obligated to Larry because he had gone all the way to Bend in central Oregon to help her move.

She kept putting Larry off until one day she said, "Okay, I'm going on Friday night to pick up some friends at the airport. If he wants to meet me at the airport, that's fine."

I told Larry, "That's bullshit. Either it's a legitimate date or nothing."

Larry went back to Kathy. The only way she'd go out with me was if we double dated. Larry picked her up and brought her over to the moorage. He introduced me to Kathy and said, "This is your date for tonight. We'll meet you over at the restaurant." He and his girlfriend left, Kathy hopped into my truck, and we drove to The Castle in Gladstone.

We had so much fun. The restaurant was nice. We were laughing, telling jokes, and having such a good time the waitress had to come over and ask us to tone it down. It was a little embarrassing at thirty-five having the waitress tell you to be quieter. After dinner, the four of us went to a dance place on McLoughlin. Larry and his girlfriend danced and Kathy and I kept talking. It was a fun date and the beginning of a new relationship that lasts to this day.

Chapter 41: Raise These Boys

THE WEEK after our first date I called Kathy, but she couldn't go out because she was on call for the OR. Instead, she invited me over for dinner. I think it was a Saturday.

When I went to dinner I met her sons, Chris and Mike. Mike was seven and Chris was around two and a half. About seven o'clock there was a bad traffic accident on I-5. Kathy got a call from the hospital and had to go in to work. She told me she would take the boys to the babysitter. Well, I remembered when I was a little kid—I hated going to the sitter because your parents would wake you up in the middle of the night to go home. I told her that, if it was okay, I'd watch the kids, put them to bed, and then sack out on the couch. I could go home when she came back.

She agreed. Mike and I got out a game and Chris played on the floor. About nine o'clock, I told Mike to pick up the toys; it was time to go to bed. As I was sitting back on the couch watching Mike pick up toys and Chris playing on the floor, I was thinking about what was going to happen to Kathy and those two boys. I'd always figured I'd never get married again; I was so focused on my own life that there wasn't much room for another person. This caused problems in my first marriage and the situation hadn't changed. I had just met them, but I have a big soft spot for kids.

I was sitting there thinking about this and how Kathy and I would probably date until we found the differences in each other and drift apart, just like any normal relationship. Kathy would probably meet someone at the hospital and they'd put this family back together again. I was pretty satisfied with that conclusion and as I finished the thought, the voice hit me. It said, "You are going to raise these boys. You cannot trust that responsibility to another man."

Well, I'd dealt with that voice before and knew you didn't argue with it. This was the longest voice message I received and, unlike the other voice messages, it was quite specific. I thought, *Wow, what am I going to do?* I hardly knew Kathy. I'd only met her the week before. And here I was being told I've got to raise these two boys. What did it mean? I simply knew I was going to marry her. At the time, I'd kissed Kathy one time on our first date. It was a strange position, knowing I was going to marry this woman and I didn't really know her. I decided the best thing to do was to let the relationship take its course. A year later, we did decide to get married. I adopted Mike and Chris and raised them. The voice was right again.

This was the longest message I received. When the voice speaks, they do not give any detail. It is up to you to figure it out what the messages mean. I had to figure out where does "man" come from? I determined the voice meant the men Kathy might bring into her life and into the life of these boys that these men might not be good for them.

When I met Kathy and the voice told me I was going the raise these boys, and I knew I was going to marry her, I looked back over my life and realized I'd need to change some things. I hadn't always been perfect. I made a pledge to myself to never touch another woman romantically. I enjoy hugs and kisses, but that's friendship. I never broke that pledge.

Chapter 42: The Cocohead

THE *COCOHEAD* was a barge I salvaged twice—once when I worked for Devine's and later for another small company. The first time it went aground was around Eureka, California—a Foss Tug lost it in a winter storm and we went down with the *Salvage Chief*, patched it up, and pulled it off the beach.

To keep the salvaged barge afloat while the *Chief* towed it back to Portland, Mick Leitz and I were in the hold with some of the crew from the *Chief* keeping an eye on the patches we'd put on to make sure the barge didn't try to sink while under tow. It was December and the project had been cold and grueling. Down in the dark, cold hull, the trip up the Oregon coast was cold and boring; we slept in sleeping bags and ate cold food out of boxes. On New Year's Eve we were at or near the Columbia River; there was a break in the weather and Captain Reino on the *Chief* had the ship's helicopter fly over to us with supplies.

Mick and I ignored the food treats and went straight for the two bottles of whiskey; we didn't share with the crew. After all, we deserved it: Mick and I had done all the hard work the month we spent in the cold December surf salvaging the *Cocohead.* We were still a little keyed up from successfully finishing a hard job and feeling pretty proud of the knowledge that, under the conditions, only *we* could have pulled off this salvage job.

Once the whiskey had time to go into effect, Mick got to wondering who was the better fighter, him or me. Mick was a little shorter than me, but stockier. I said, "Go for it." He hit me, but with my training at Grandpa's boxing gym, I'd learned at a young age how to roll with a punch. Mick hadn't had the same training and my punch knocked him flat. We still laugh about it today.

The second time I was called to salvage the *Cocohead* was after I left Devine's. On the way to Alaska, a small towing company lost the *Cocohead* in Canadian waters—they cut a corner too sharp and hit a rock, creating a hole in the side. The *Cocohead* had a full house on deck making it unstable. Now the *Cocohead* was upside down in an inlet in Canada. The tow company hired a Canadian company to salvage it.

Two diver friends of mine had a small salvage company. They heard I had quit Devine's and asked me if I'd go in with them as a third partner. I wasn't real excited about the idea, but I'd just met Kathy and I wasn't sure yet what I was supposed to be doing. I decided to give it a try.

I had recently taken Kathy on a trip to California to meet my relatives. I was out of shape from not doing anything. That and driving long distances caused me to blow a disk in my back and I ended up in the hospital where Kathy worked. Those were the days when they cut all the muscle around the disk. It took months to heal. While Kathy nursed me through the healing process, I went into partnership with these two guys, not knowing what I was going to do with my life. I didn't have to buy into the partnership—they just wanted my reputation and skills.

The *Cocohead* project seemed like a way to fill the time until I had a clearer picture of what I was supposed to do. The *Cocohead* had wing tanks, bottom tanks, and rake tanks. The main body was the cargo area. The deck had a house and 25-foot hatches to lower cargo into the hold.

The Canadian company hired to salvage the barge called our little company and wanted me to come up to survey the wreck and give a recommendation on what to do. I flew up, swam around the barge, and got a good feel for what needed to be done to salvage it. The exercise was good for my back injury.

The same ship we used on the Aleutian job, the *Sudbury*, was in the area and we used it for our salvage platform

During a meeting with the underwriters' rep and other people in the industry involved with the accident, I was asked to give my thoughts. My first statement was, "I recommend that you secure the deck cargo of lumber and tow the barge to Vancouver, (British Columbia) into a controlled environment, for the rolling process."

The Canadian company wanted to roll the barge over, with the deck house still attached, in the cove where the vessel lay. The cove was in a wilderness area; the bottom had large, jagged rocks, and there was no place to touch bottom. The *Sudbury* didn't have the equipment needed to roll the barge. I suggested the Canadians burn the house off in sections, drop the pieces to the bottom, roll the barge, pick up the pieces, and stack them on the deck for the company that owned the barge to reassemble. The Canadian company's rep told me, in front of the group, that if we did it my way the pieces would warp and never go back on. That didn't make sense. He was lying, but I didn't know why.

A young U.S. Salvage rep, whom I knew well and who previously worked under Doc Stream (the underwriter who told me 'don't touch bottom'), jumped up, slammed his fist on the table, and said, "I'm damn sick and tired of being told to tow this vessel to Vancouver! Upside down!"

I had no idea why he felt that way—this was the first time I'd said it. (Ironically, they eventually did just that, but not before I got fed up with the entire project.)

I said, "I was hired to give you my best advice and that's my best advice. If you try to roll it here, the offsetting weight of the house and the movement of the unknown weights internally in the barge could cause a lot of problems. It's going to be very risky to roll it where it is."

The rep's anger was strange to me—they had asked me to take a look at the situation and give them my recommendation. I had salvaged the same barge before and was familiar with the layout. Based on the way it was loaded, the barge was built like a ship with wing walls and double bottom tanks. There was cargo inside the barge and a load of logs on the deck. It's very difficult to roll a barge over when it has deck cargo. The deck cargo had to come off. The deck house needed to come off, too.

In the meeting, it was decided to have the Canadian company do the salvage and I would act as consultant. They would pay me $330 a day. Due to visa restrictions, I couldn't dive for hire in Canada, but I could go down and have a look at the project as it progressed. Like a fool, I took their offer.

The Canadian salvage company hired the largest diving company on the west coast of Canada to do the actual diving work. They showed up with several divers, tenders and helpers. I instantly recognized they were very unskilled salvage divers. I tried to communicate with them, but they were arrogant and belligerent and didn't want anything to do with me. We bunked together on the *Sudbury* for a month or so and I just could not communicate with them, particularly the older divers. The younger divers were learning the trade and, on the side, they would talk to me. I tried to explain to them some of the things they needed to know.

One part of the project called for sealing the huge deck hatches, which were underwater and under the barge. Under the terms of the project, I was to tell the dive company what to do and the divers would do the work, but they wouldn't take instruction. After a couple of days, the deck hatches were still not sealed.

I told my tender to have my gear ready at lunchtime when the other divers went below deck of the *Sudbury* to eat. Once they were out of sight, I jumped into the water and put the seal on the deck hatches properly and started the pumps. By the end of lunchtime, when the divers came back on deck, the barge had raised a couple of feet. That upset them, but at least we got that part of the job done.

Another day when the hired divers were at lunch, I burned a hole that had to be done perfectly. It was where we were going to attach a big block for the parbuckle. I got caught coming out of the water. "What do you think you're doing?" the lead diver challenged me. "You can't dive on our project."

I explained the importance of the accuracy of this particular hole; that rolling the barge safely depended on it. He kept shooting off his mouth, saying they could burn and blah, blah, blah.

When he wound down a bit, I told him, "You're the one that shouldn't talk, because you are the worst of all. You can't burn. The other day I was watching you while you were cutting off the pipe stanchions. You're scared of the electric arc." I let that sink in. "I offered to teach you how to burn, but you're too arrogant. You won't let me teach you. That's why I did it myself."

That confrontation just pushed us further apart.

Before the rolling process, I instructed the divers that when they put the camlock fittings (used to attach the air and dewatering hoses) on the barge, they had to wire the ears of the camlock to secure them in place. They assured me they would.

Near the end of the time we were pumping air into the barge, which normally goes on 24 hours a day until there is enough air inside to roll the vessel over, the tide started to drop. It was after dark when we had the vessel on its edge and ready to roll, but the tide was still dropping. We decided to wait until morning when the tide was back in to continue the roll. In the meantime, the tugs would maintain pull so we wouldn't lose any progress.

During the night there was a huge explosion and the barge went back upside down. In the morning, I dove down to see what had gone wrong. The bow compartment had a three inch camlock fitting that wasn't wired and it had come loose. When the air hose came off, the bow compartment flooded, putting a terrible strain on the lines and a cable to the tug broke. The large steel D socket on the end of the cable went like a bullet right through one of the six-inch steel pipes used to form tie-up bits. Thankfully, no one was hurt.

We had to go back and start again.

Between attempts to roll the barge, it was decided everybody should take a break and go home for a week or so to get some rest. I promised myself I wouldn't come back. In that week the Canadian company hired to salvage the barge bought the barge "as is, where is." It was quite a relief, except for the fact that at that point the attempt was a failure. It was my first failure and it hurt.

When they were ready to salvage the barge, the Canadian company sent a guy down to plead with me to come back on the job. I asked him who would be in charge. "I will," he said.

I told him, "No."

The barge had all the plumbing needed for the salvage job already in it. I laid out what they needed to do, but I wouldn't go back up. I think they set up the project for failure so they could get a barge cheap.

They ended up doing just what I originally suggested—cut off the house and towed it upside down to Vancouver to roll it over.

I think the lesson here is that I gave up control. I feel strongly that I am a puppet to the spiritual world, that they use me to accomplish their ends. I am not in control of those situations. However, I have a strong need to be in control where man is involved. If I'm not in control of the situation, how can the spiritual use me to accomplish their ends?

Chapter 43: Big Break

LATER IN the new partnership, sometime in 1977, I went on a job for a barge that capsized and sank inside the mouth of the Columbia River. A man from Seattle had the salvage rights and he wanted to set up a salvage operation, but he didn't have any equipment and wanted to rent our crane barge; we had to deliver it to the job site on Clatsop Spit inside Buoy 14.

I was still healing from my back surgery. I agreed to go down with a deckhand and the partner who ran the tug. We were hoping to get there before the tide changed, but we got a late start and had to fight the incoming tide. As we pulled up to the sunken barge, the tide changed and we suddenly found ourselves in surf caused by the out-flowing river and the incoming tide piling the seas up in the low water at the spit.

We were using the tug to push the barge. All of a sudden, we had a large swell, causing the tug to jump up onto the barge—it looked like a bull mating a cow. The tug and crane barge were still connected with winch cables, only now the tug was hung up on the crane barge. In order to back the tug off the crane barge and free ourselves, we had to get the cables loose. The two other guys went forward to undo the cables, and I went for one of the hand winches. It had a big T handle. As I got the dog—the piece that holds the drum in place—out from the lock and drum, the sea hit us diagonally from the side. It shoved the tug hard the wrong way, which tightened the cable fiddle tight and jerked the winch handle from my hand.

The T handle started spinning like a blur and hit my leg. As I was falling face first into the handle, I thought, *Well, I bit it; this is the end.* It was like slow motion. I was getting whack, whack, whacked by this handle and, suddenly, I was airborne. The winch tossed me across fifteen feet of deck into the river and sea swell.

I bobbed to the surface. My first thought was, *Wow, that wasn't bad. I better get back to the boat; they're going to miss me.* My partner and the deckhand were on the other side of the tug trying to disconnect the barge; they didn't know I was gone.

Fortunately, I was wearing a float coat, which is a buoyant work coat. I rarely wore one. It was a warm day, making it particularly unusual for me to have it on. I had thought about taking it off. I don't know why I left it on—it was another example of when it seemed someone was looking out for me.

I saw the 16-foot aluminum skiff we kept tied alongside the tug and figured I'd better get to it. I took a big kick and stroke and it was like my left leg was just flying in the breeze. I thought, *Well, that's broken, but the other one's okay.* I swam over to the skiff, pulled myself out of the water, and lay across the seat of the skiff. The skiff was being jerked back and forth with the swells and my broken leg started to really hurt with each motion.

I hollered for my partner. He finally came over and saw me lying in the skiff with blood running down my leg. I instructed him to stay on the tug deck and reach down to get hold of my arms and for the deckhand to come around and get hold of my legs and pick them up.

I said, "Get me aboard the tug—no matter what I do or say, just get me aboard the tug." I knew the pain would damn near kill me. Away they went and I started screaming. When they got me aboard, I told the deckhand to get two pieces of wood and some rags to stabilize my leg. We were still getting hit by swells from the side and I couldn't stand the grinding the bones made every time the tug moved. The deckhand put a compress on the open wound and two sticks alongside the leg, tightening rags around the sticks and my leg to stabilize the break. In the meantime, the tug and crane barge were still tangled, and we couldn't leave until the crane barge was secured.

A Coast Guard boat came by towing a small boat. I told my partner to call the Coast Guard boat operator and tell him there's a man that's been injured with a compound fracture that's bleeding and who has been thrown into the water. My partner called and the Coast Guard came back with, "We cannot assist you. We have a boat in tow."

They were towing a small boat. They could have anchored it, come over and gotten me, and picked up the small boat. But that wasn't in the procedure.

I said to my partner, "Call the Coast Guard base in Astoria and ask them to send a helicopter."

He did that and they said, "We cannot assist you. We do not have a pilot for the helicopter."

The Ilwaco Coast Guard Station was listening to all this. They piped in and said, "We can come get you with a boat."

Ilwaco was just across the river on the Washington side.

I said, "Okay. Fine. Do it."

Going to Ilwaco almost lost me my leg.

The Coast Guard boat arrived in about half an hour. They took me aboard and put me in an inflatable cast. Boy, it felt good. Away we went to Ilwaco.

When they got me to the hospital in Ilwaco, the doctor said, "We've got to get an x-ray of that leg."

They put me on the x-ray table, cut off my pants, took my boots off, and x-rayed the break. After the films were developed, the doctor came in and said, "It's a pretty nasty break. It's going to be painful to move you. Instead, we'll set it right here on the table."

The doctor had this big nurse. She grabbed hold of my shoulders and held me down while the doctor grabbed my leg, which was laying off to the left. He elongated my leg, and then started rotating the foot upright. I started screaming again. Finally, the doctor released the pressure and let the bones go back into place. I looked up and my left foot was at a fifteen or twenty-degree angle.

I told him, "A little more to the right, Doc."

Away we went again. Another big scream. He released my leg and my left foot was now pretty much lined up with my right foot. The doctor got out the plaster of Paris and put a cast from my hip down to my foot. By now it was afternoon.

The doctor said, "I'm going to leave a hole in the cast right over the hole in your leg so we can observe it."

It sounded like a good idea. By the time he got that done, it was five or six o'clock. He said goodbye and told me he'd see me in the morning.

A nurse wheeled me to a room and put me into bed. It was a small hospital with fifteen or so beds. I was lying there thinking, *There's no way I'm going to be able to sleep. There's too much pain. Fact is, the pain is getting worse.* There wasn't a call button. I started yelling. No one came. I was getting pretty desperate. There was a little table next to the bed with a pitcher of water. I thought, *I can take that pitcher of water and throw it; I think I can break the window in the door and get someone's attention.*

I was just about ready to let fly with the pitcher when a nurse came storming down the hall and into the room. She was pissed because I'd been yelling for quite a while. She said, "What's the matter with you?"

I said, "Lady, there's no way I can get to sleep because I have too much pain. Can you give me something for it?"

She said, "Haven't you had your shots?"

I said, "I haven't had anything since I entered this hospital."

She grabbed the chart off the end of the bed and read it. Her face dropped. No pain shots. Nothing. I hadn't even had an aspirin yet. She called the doctor and got permission to give me a shot. It knocked me out.

I woke up the next morning. My partner had called Kathy and told her what happened. Ilwaco is about a two-hour drive from Tualatin. She showed up early in the morning. Kathy is tall, six feet. She strode into the room, threw the sheet back, and demanded to know, "What'd they do?"

I said, "They set my leg."

She said, "It's not been washed out. It's bleeding. It's a mess."

At the time, Kathy was working as an operating room (OR) nurse in Tualatin (near Portland) and could see what needed to be done. She grabbed the phone, called the hospital where she worked, and got the surgeon on duty. She explained the situation to him.

He told her, "Kathy, stay with him. We'll send an ambulance. When he gets here, we'll operate."

A couple of hours later, the ambulance arrived and away we went.

At Meridian Park Hospital I was put under sedation and the surgeon operated on my leg, cleaned out the mess, and put the bones back together. When I came out of anesthesia, the doctor came into my room and said, "Ken, you really had a bad break and it was dirty for so long, you're likely going to lose your leg. Prepare yourself for that."

I was glad to be alive. I could handle that.

Fortunately, it never infected. I was kept full of antibiotics and, slowly, my leg healed. I was in a full leg cast for six months. When they removed the cast, I thought I was okay, but after a few days of walking on it I noticed my leg was bending. It had broken right below the knee joint in a porous area. According to the x-rays, the bones were knitted back together, but the bone tissue was still soft.

The surgeon went back in, cut a wedge out of the bone and put in a staple. I was back in a full leg cast for another six months. But I kept my leg. I have to give Kathy credit for that. If it hadn't been for Kathy, I would have lost it.

I've been asked if I sued the Ilwaco hospital. I was too busy to think about suing the hospital. I made my deepest dive with that cast. I didn't think to get my new work boots when I left the first hospital. I never got them back. That's what I should have sued them for.

Chapter 44: Diver Lost

AFTER I left Devine's, I did another job for the same mill we had so much trouble with before. I was in a full leg cast and couldn't dive. Cliff Larson, my tender, wanted to be a professional diver. The job was to inspect part of the equipment in an underground building full of effluent—just look, feel, and report. Nothing technical.

There were compartments and tunnels running in all directions. All of the pumps running off this compartment were to be locked and sealed by the head of maintenance before we went into the water. He assured us they were all locked out. There was so much noise from the mill operations that we couldn't tell ourselves if it had been done.

Cliff was using tanks, so his air was self-contained. He needed to go through several hatches and compartments to get to the spot we were inspecting. The space in the compartments was completely black and full of water. I sent him down with a hand line attached to his wrist that would allow him to find his way back to the entrance point.

As Cliff swam through the pipes, I gently let out the hand line.

All of a sudden, the line ripped from my hands. I had no more connection with my diver. We learned a pump was running. The tug I felt on the line wasn't Cliff moving toward the site, it was a pump off one of the tunnels sucking on the line. It sucked the line into the propellers, jerking the line out of my hand and off the diver's wrist.

Cliff was under the floor in a dark complex of tunnels full of water with no air, except what he carried on his back, and no line back to the entrance.

Now I had to decide whether or not to send in Bud, our backup diver. For all I knew, Cliff has been sucked into the pump, too. I had made up my mind to put Bud in the water to see if he could find Cliff when Cliff poked his head out of the pipe opening. Fortunately, he had figured his way back out. He had a big grin on his face. Knowing you have defeated death is a great feeling.

That mill was a disaster and it was lucky we never lost anyone.

It was our last job for that mill. We worked for the Engineering department and the head of engineering was an absolute idiot. We were in a meeting with his boss and his engineering staff when he started blaming me for the issues with this job and the previous one with the temporary dam we built that almost broke from the rainwater runoff the mill let come down toward us. I laid it all out to him, his boss, and his staff.

"You're the failure," I said. "You've failed us on every instance. Everything that went wrong was your responsibility. You were to make sure pumps were turned off. You selected the kid to man the pump (that was to remove the rainwater runoff). You gave us toxic glue. It's a miracle you haven't killed us."

The room went silent. I left and never went back.

The Crown Simpson paper mill was just down the beach and we did all kinds of work for them with no problems. What we needed, we asked for and they did it. Why there was such a huge difference between two similar operations is hard to understand.

Chapter 45: Brother Jonathan

THE PADDLE steamer *Brother Jonathon*[27] had quite a bit of treasure, mostly gold, on board when it went down in a storm July 30, 1865, off Crescent City, California. It struck a submerged pinnacle now known as Jonathan Rock on St. George Reef, also known as the Dragon's Teeth.

There was a professor down in Eureka whom I had met when I was working on the pipelines at the mills who had been looking into the history of the *Brother Jonathan*. The treasure-laden wreck had been looked for by other groups over the years. In 1977 it was our turn.

The professor and some other people he knew set up the Brother Jonathan Corporation. The professor and his group didn't have any money so the corporation hired us to do the search on a share basis. We made a share arrangement with a fisherman, Keith Richcreek, out of Crescent City, to use his 60-foot fishing boat as a dive platform. The professor only went on a couple of dives; he got seasick very easily.

Brother Jonathan

I kind of headed up our end of the venture. The idea started prior to breaking my leg. I recruited three other divers: Dick Long, Connie Schweiger, and Bud Sanders. Dick worked for a competitor of Devine's, Connie ran a dive shop, and Bud had been in partnership with one of my two current dive partners.

---

[27] *Brother Jonathan* was a paddle steamer that crashed on an uncharted rock near Point St. George, off the coast of Crescent City, California, on 30 July 1865. The ship was carrying 244 passengers and crew with a large shipment of gold. Only 19 survived the wreck, making it the deadliest shipwreck up to that time on the Pacific Coast of the United States. Although accounts vary, inspection of the passenger and crew list supports the number of 244 passenger and crew lost with 19 people surviving. She was named after Brother Jonathan, a character personifying the United States before the creation of Uncle Sam… No human remains were ever found. In 1996, a mini-sub scooted past a "glint" on the bottom, raising curiosity. On 30 August 1996, divers found gold coins and on that expedition recovered 875 1860s gold coins in near-mint condition. Over time, the salvers recovered 1,207 gold coins, primarily $20 Double Eagles, in addition to numerous artifacts.
http://en.wikipedia.org/wiki/Brother_Jonathan_(steamer)
http://shipwrecks.slc.ca.gov/Brother_Jonathan/Brother_Jonathan_Default.html

We concentrated our search area in the 170 to 200-foot-deep water around Jonathan Rock. I made some of my deeper dives looking for this treasure ship. The deepest dive of my career was 190-feet with a helmet and surface-supplied air, in totally black water, with a full leg cast. It wasn't my smartest move. I used soap to slip the cast into my dry suit.

On one of our dives, we were making circular search patterns in the deep water around Jonathan Rock. We didn't have a decompression chamber and were using tanks, not helmets, so we tied an extra tank and regulator to the anchor buoy we were working off of for the divers to use for their rest stops when surfacing.

Bud was the eldest of the divers. He went into the service in World War II at age fifteen and was one of the original Navy Frogmen. Bud went down to make his circle. The water happened to be clear that day. He was on a set of double tanks and trying to cover as much area as he could. He was out on a 100-foot search line across the bottom and swimming hard when he realized he had run out of air—he could feel the drag on his regulator.

Bud needed to decompress—he couldn't go straight to the surface without the risk of getting the bends. To get to the spare tank, Bud swam along the bottom and followed his search line back to the anchor and came up the anchor line. But by the time he got to the reserve tank, he didn't think he had time to stop and change regulators—take one out of his mouth, put in the other one, and turn the spare tank on—so he just went up the anchor line to the surface.

The air in a diver's lungs expands as he comes out of the pressure of deep water, but Bud was already so starved for oxygen that, even though he was coming up fast, he wasn't getting enough air to sustain himself. A diver steadily exhales a bit all the way to the surface to keep the expanding bubbles from bursting his lungs. We didn't have any communication with Bud so we had no idea of the trouble he was in, but we could see his bubbles boiling and we knew something was wrong. We pulled the boat we were using for a dive platform over to the buoy. The boat had a rubber boat tied alongside. When Bud hit the surface, he grabbed the buoy and wouldn't let loose. We pulled him up over the side and into the rubber boat. He was lying upside down in the bottom.

I was hollering at him, "Bud, what's wrong? What's wrong?"

I wanted to know what was happening. Then I realized he still had his mouthpiece in his mouth, his mask was on, and he wasn't breathing. He was unconscious. I jerked out his mouthpiece and broke the seal on his mask and took it off, exposing his nose to the air. He let out a big gasp and came to.

We didn't have a decompression chamber so we had to decompress Bud by putting him back in the water. (Normally, a diver will decompress in the water, taking rest stops at various depths during the ascent in order to gradually release the nitrogen stored in the blood during deep dives. Without these decompression stops, the nitrogen compressed in the blood by the high pressure of a deep dive will expand and cause pain in the joints and possibly death.) We hauled anchor and headed for shore as fast as we could. We didn't want to put Bud down in deep water. If anything went wrong, it would be easier to deal with it in shallower water. We rushed him into thirty feet of water, dropped anchor, and threw him back into the water with a new tank so he could go to the bottom and decompress. He was there about an hour. Fortunately, he had no problems, no pains.

Later in the day we were celebrating that we hadn't killed anybody and Bud told us that he had actually passed out on the way up. He didn't remember hitting the buoy, he grabbed it on instinct.

He said, "The next thing I remember, I came to and my eyes opened. I saw a seagull. I knew I wasn't dead because I knew they wouldn't allow seagulls in hell."

We drove down to Crescent City four or five times to search for the *Brother Jonathan* treasure. On one dive the water was so black we couldn't see our hands on our masks. I was still diving in a full leg cast. Not being able to see or kick, I relied on a tow motor to move around on my search circle. It was tough. I had a marker buoy with me with a locator line attached to it, but the buoy collapsed and I got tangled in the line. While trying to get untangled, I got nitrogen narcosis. It was like being drunk at the bottom of the sea in complete darkness.

Connie and Dick on the deck were talking to me via the full face scuba mask communication system I was wearing and realized I was having problems. They pulled me to the surface by the safety cable, skipping the rest stops, and put me in the decompression chamber. After Bud's incident it seemed like a good idea to have one on board. It's better to decompress in a chamber than in the water because you have full control over the diver. Kathy was with us that time and got into the chamber with me. It's boring in there and it was nice to have her with me.

The boat we used had side scan sonar, which we dragged all over looking for signs of the wreck, but we didn't have the electronics they have today, and we were always on a tight budget. We never found the *Brother Jonathan*, but we did find another wreck and spent a long time playing with that. It was just a big old steel ship that was all flattened out with engines and parts spread out over the sea floor, but it satisfied the need to see a wreck.

The *Brother Jonathan* was found by Deep Sea Research Inc. in 1993, further offshore from where we were looking. The damaged ship probably drifted as it sank. I saw videotapes of the wreck. It's well preserved, nearly intact. I don't know whether anything has ever been done with it.

When you find a treasure ship—a sunken ship with valuables on it—you usually end up broke. That's because the government gets involved, prior owners get involved, insurance companies get involved, local jurisdictions get involved, and pretty soon the ones who found the ship are in court.[28] When it's over, you are broke. That's how most treasure hunts end up. Searching for the *Brother Jonathan* satisfied my need for treasure hunting. I got it out of my blood. We disbanded the corporation that was set up to look for the *Brother Jonathan* and we went about our lives.

---

[28] This case was no different. To read the court documents about ownership of the Brother Jonathan treasure go to: http://supreme.justia.com/cases/federal/us/523/491/

Chapter 46: Foam Floatation

AFTER BREAKING my leg, I decided I was being given the message to get away from the salvage business. I had tried to do that when I left Devine's. The year I worked as a partner in the small diving business felt like going backwards. The broken leg confirmed it was time to go. I sold my interest to my other two partners. I was finished with the salvage business—for the second time.

It was 1978 and I was married to Kathy. We had just remodeled the little Sportcraft Landing restaurant on the old Boone's Ferry barge into a home and were living there. Our overhead was low and it was a good time to start another business.

For some time I'd had an idea in my head for a method of installing flotation foam under docks and buildings.

The foam business idea was the change in the tunnel of my life that I'd envisioned back in 1969. I can see now this change was laid out ahead of time, waiting for me to take it. I was still diving, but making better money; money that allowed me to get ahead and build two new moorages. I think the successes in my professional life were the spiritual world's way of compensating me for the challenges in my personal life.

In those days, floating structures were built on large floating logs. Over time, logs with the added weight of a structure on them got water logged and sat lower in the water. Eventually, the logs sank. To keep structures afloat, solid foam was placed under the logs to raise the structure to the desired height.

The traditional method for installing flotation foam involved several people with small pontoon barges and what looked like an upside-down conveyor belt with buckets on it. As the buckets rotated down into the water, the bucket grabbed a barrel-shaped piece of foam and forced it down to the end of the conveyor, which was in the water under the building or dock. When it came to the end of the conveyor, the bucket turned loose the foam log and the foam would slam up underneath the structure. It wasn't very precise. If there was too much space between the logs, the foam log went up into the floor; the force of the foam would hit the floor joist and push the floor up and once it was in place, you couldn't get it out again. It was chaos.

It was also expensive. Using traditional methods, the pontoon needed to pull alongside the structure. A floating home has electric service, telephone, water, and sewage lines attached to it that had to be disconnected. It was quite an operation and took an entire day to disconnect the services, pull the home away from the dock, install the foam, reconnect the structure to the dock, and reconnect the services.

My idea was for a diver to take a ballasted tank, strap a round block of foam to it, submerge the tank by letting the air out—allowing lead ballast to make the tank almost neutral, then shut the vents off, and push the tank underneath the building. Since the tank had only a few pounds of positive buoyancy, a diver could manually push the tank underneath the structure, de-ballast the tank by opening a valve—which put air back into the tank to float it into exact position, take the straps off the foam, take the tank back out, and go get another block of foam. Because we were not limited in how far under the structure we could reach, we did not have to disconnect the house and disrupt things. The new method was less expensive, faster, and more precise.

I was healing from my leg injury and as soon as I got out of the second cast I took a couple of steel 50-gallon drums, welded them together end-to-end, and built a tank to try my theory.

Bob Lamphere, the car dealership owner, was a good friend of Evan Hale, who lived in a floating home at Sportcraft. We were having a drink one night and Bob was complaining that a new boathouse he'd hauled up the river to his property above Wilsonville needed flotation. I told him about my new idea and he kept hounding me to get to it. So away we went. Kathy and I took our skiff with the tank and a bunch of foam logs up the Willamette River and that was our first test. It was a success.

I contacted some people in the Jantzen Beach area, where there are many docks and float homes, and explained what I was doing. They wanted me to come down to put foam under their houses and we set a date. Kathy was sick that day so I took my dad along as tender. We foamed three houses in three or four hours. All the time I was foaming I was thinking about the improvements I could make on the tank. By the time I got out of the water, I had a better design in my head. Dad and I loaded the boat and went down the river to a little fabrication company. I drew a sketch for the guy and had him build me a tank. The tank is the same design we use today. When I eventually had to build a new tank, except for a minor change in the way the ballast goes in and out, the new one is identical. It still works perfectly.

At first, I used the same foam logs everyone else used, but they were not good quality. After building the new tank and proving it was a viable business, I wanted to better control the quality of the logs. I studied how to build a foam mold out of aluminum, built a mold, took it to a plant in Kent, Washington, and installed the mold there. Our agreement was that they could only use the mold to build my foam. The new design was blocks with rounded edges that didn't roll. (Later, the environmental rules changed and we had to encapsulate the foam in plastic.)

Our reputation spread by word of mouth. After the first year in the foam business Kathy and I took a vacation to check out a rumor I'd heard that a resort on Lake Mead was having trouble keeping their buildings afloat. The place was huge. We went to the café for breakfast and I was looking at the buildings and it was a mess—the doors didn't close properly, the windows were jammed, the floats were at different elevations, and in many places there wasn't much reserve buoyancy. I asked the waitress where to find the marina manager; I told her I wanted to talk to him. He was in another booth and after his breakfast came over to our booth. Kathy and I introduced ourselves and I said, "We're in the floatation business."

I saw his eyes light up. He sat down and we had a nice visit. He hired us on the spot, asking "How soon can you do it?"

We went down to Nevada a month later. I took two of my old diving partners, Connie, who was on the *Brother Jonathan* treasure hunt, and Larry (both were eventually my business partners in Scappoose Moorage).

The Lake Mead Marina had a huge floating building with two restaurants, a bar, rental shops, docks, and ice making equipment and it was all sinking. It was also coming apart.

We got there before the marina opened and made an upside-down blueprint of the load distribution—we had to measure where all the heavy galley equipment (stoves, ice machine, ice storage, etc.) was located, plus bearing walls, and so on. We were in the water by nine o'clock.

Connie and Larry brought down the foam, which had been delivered earlier by truck. Kathy acted as tender while I dove. About two-thirty the first afternoon I asked Kathy to figure out how much foam we had put under. She said it was about 170 blocks. We were going too fast. The resort was feeding us, putting us up in nice rooms, and the weather was beautiful. It was cold and miserable at home. The resort was pleased with what we were doing, so I had both Connie and Larry put their gear on and directed them to put foam under all the load bearing walls, telling them, "Don't go too fast."

It was a hell of a job. Fun, but hot. I was wearing cutoffs and a tee-shirt, no wetsuit, and I was comfortable. But in the hundred-degree sun Kathy was only comfortable when we were on the shady side of a building. Even then she was miserable, but we were making good money and she liked that.

By the end of the first day we had 200 blocks of foam under the structure with only 140 left to go. In three-and-a-half days we put in 340 blocks of foam. Normally, the foam we had built using our mold was 12 cubic feet with 740 pounds of lift. Rather than haul our foam to California, we had special foam blocks made locally that were 10 cubic feet with 600 pounds of lift. This raised the building a total of seven inches. It was all level—the doors would open; the windows would open.

The same company was building a brand-new facility at the other end of the lake. It was a screwed-up design and about two-thirds built when they called me down. They built a huge ice making facility, but hadn't allowed for the extra weight of the water or ice. I fixed that by putting more foam in the right places. As they built the structure, I made several trips down to Nevada and corrected the floatation until it was stable.

For the next three years we installed foam all over the West Coast, with many projects in the Portland area. In the first two years of the operation we averaged sixty foam blocks a day for every day we went out. I couldn't keep up and had to hire Larry and Connie to relieve me.

During the first year, eight people tried to copy my patented system, but none of them could make it work properly. There are other people who use a weight with a quick release and a diver pulls the release. The weight falls to the bottom of the river and they winch it back up. It's more difficult to position and move foam with that system.

Of course, my system wasn't completely trouble free. We were working in 40 to 50 feet of water and I was installing foam with my newly-designed ballast tank. Larry was tending me. I was letting the air out and the water in to make the tank heavy so I could loosen a strap around a foam log that had gotten stuck, but miscalculated and the strap came loose, letting the foam log loose. I didn't have enough time to add air to the tank and the tank sank fast.

Normally, I'd dive down and, after the tank settled on the bottom, add air to bring it back up. This time the tank gear hooked onto my dive gear and took me down to the bottom with it. I had some congestion in one ear and the eardrum ruptured. I was on the bottom of the river in dark water tangled with the tank and an overwhelming sensation of tumbling end over end down the river when logic said I wasn't moving at all. I had to overpower the sense of tumbling with my mind. I added air to the tank and it went up underneath the building we had been working on. As I rose toward the surface, the tumbling effect slowed. When I came to the surface, I was under the floating home and I still had vertigo. I knew the logs under the house weren't really moving and that if I went along the side of them, I'd eventually get out from underneath the house. I left the tank and followed the logs hand over hand until I got to the dock alongside the house. In my head I was still tumbling—I could feel the dock moving, but I knew it wasn't, and I pulled myself out. The tumbling stopped. It was a wild ride.

To repair the tear in my eardrum the doctor took a patch of graft skin from my shoulder. You can't sew or glue skin to the eardrum so I asked him how we was going to attach it. He drew me a picture. You want the patch on the inside of the tear. To get there he cut through the bottom of the ear canal and came up behind the torn eardrum with the skin graft. To hold the patch in place he filled the inner ear with a dissolvable putty. The graft took, but I never regained full hearing in that ear.

My other ear is equally damaged. I was welding on a job and a red bead of molten steel went into my ear. Talk about jumping around shaking your head trying to get rid of it! I had to dive later and didn't know I'd burned a hole in my eardrum. I went to equalize my ears by plugging my nose and blowing and found I could blow air out of my ear. It was a small hole and I don't remember exactly how we fixed that one, but I do remember that I couldn't dive for a while. I knew the eardrum was healed when I couldn't blow air out of it anymore.

Some of the professional divers I knew seemed to think installing foam was demeaning. After all, I had been at the top of the salvage diving field. They didn't realize that I was making more money with the foam business than I ever had as a salvage diver. I could charge the same rates as other foam companies, but my system allowed us to do three or four times more work in the same amount of time.

In the mid 1990's I turned over that part of the business to my son, Eric, and today it's part of his dock building business.

Chapter 47: Dredging for Gold

I TOOK a break from the foam business to take my sailboat, the *Que Sera,* to look for gold.

I'd been searching for gold for more than 20 years. My first attempt at gold dredging was right out of high school in 1958 or 59. When Chinamen came over to the Little Applegate River area in southern Oregon, the area had a lot of gold. The gold was stuck in crevices in the river; they would suck the gold out and get rich.[29] My high school buddy and later log salvage partner, Keith Wilson, and I built a little wooden sluice box and spent several weekends on the Applegate River out of Jacksonville. We used hookah gear floating on an inner tube; we also used pans. We worked at it off and on for six months to a year, but only got a little flour gold; Keith still has a little vial of it.

On the first trip to Alaska in *Que Sera* to look for gold I took my dad and a friend named Don. Don had diabetes and got sick on the way up the Washington coast. Instead of going directly to our goal, Icy Bay, we went into Puget Sound. Don wanted to get off at Friday Harbor in the San Juan Islands. He had worked in Alaska when he was young and had a lot of memories so I knew he would be disappointed to miss the trip. I eventually convinced him to stay on; the water for the rest of trip up the Inside Passage would be flat most of the way. He stayed and the trip went well.

---

[29] The first European Americans to visit the (Little Applegate River) area were a group of fur trappers led by Peter Skene Ogden in 1827. The community of Buncom was founded by Chinese miners in 1851 when gold, silver, cinnabar (mercury), and chromite were discovered in nearby Jacksonville. In the spring of 1854, James Sterling and Aaron Davis discovered gold in the Sterling Creek area, and hundreds of miners soon arrived. The town of Sterlingville was founded, and by October its population had risen to over 1,500. Mining lasted through the 1850s and 60s, and much of the riverbeds of Sterling Creek and the lower Little Applegate River were excavated. The Sterling Ditch and several other ditches were constructed in the 1870s, providing water to large hydraulic mining operations in Sterlingville and surrounding regions. The Sterlingville mine quickly became the largest hydraulic mine in Oregon, and possibly the entire western United States. http://en.wikipedia.org/wiki/Little_Applegate_River

As recently as a half decade ago, a couple of pound sized nuggets were taken from a small tributary of the Applegate River, proof that the "big ones" are still out there if you are willing to work hard to find them. Source: Nov.12, 2011 Kerby Jackson http://www.oregongold.net/category/oregon-gold/southern-oregon-gold-oregon-gold/jackson-county-gold/applegate-river-jackson-county-gold-oregon-gold/

Don flew back from Ketchikan, where Dad and I picked up Evan Hale. Evan, a good friend a couple years younger than me, built a floating home at Sportcraft Landing. He worked for US Bank as an executive—a trouble shooter of some kind. He also had a farm in Canby. When they were tearing down one of the old US Banks, he put dibs on one of the walk-in safes. He hauled the large safe up to his place in Canby, poured it in the foundation, and it became part of the house. He put a shooting gallery in the basement and the safe became a walk-in gun cabinet.

The *Que Sera* was rigged with a dredge pump inside and a sluice box hanging over the side, but we arrived in Icy Bay too early in the spring—there were too many icebergs and we couldn't work. We anchored behind a little island. During the night the wind shifted and the icebergs came in and started grinding against the side of the boat.

Besides, you can't dig a hole in sand underwater and I couldn't get deep enough with the pump to get to a solid substrate of clay or rock where the heavy gold ore would be laying.

Evan flew back to Portland and Dad and I had a great trip bringing the *Que Sera* home.

A couple years later, when my son Eric was in his 20's, I took another trip to Icy Bay dredging for gold. There's a lot of gold in Alaska. Icy Bay is in the Gulf of Alaska right where the top of the SE Alaska panhandle and the main part of the state meet. The area is known to have gold. There's even gold in the beach sand. There are several major glaciers feeding Icy Bay. The bottom of a glacier is encrusted with gravel, rocks and sand picked up as it grinds down the mountain side. At least one of the glaciers is scraping off a mother lode of gold. As its name implies, icebergs float in Icy Bay year round. Some of the icebergs get beached on the sand where they break up, melt, and drop the ore. In winter the storm surge grinds up the ore. That's my theory. The coarse gold is heavy and settles deep in the loose glacial silt.

The suction pump was powered by *Que Sera*'s main engine. A hose went down to the end of the suction about six inches in diameter used to put sand through the sluice box. Eric and I dug a hole as deep as we could. It was very hard to dig a hole deep enough in the loose silt and sand to get to the heavier ore we wanted. The ore was there, sitting on clay or a rock shelf, but underwater the loose sand filled in the hole faster than we could get to the heavier ore.

Every day we'd clean the sluice box and only get color. Finally, we decided we didn't have the right equipment to get down as deep as we needed to find ore. After a couple weeks of diving with the suction hose we were sitting in the boat and made the decision to go home. We had one little vial of gold dust.

Eric asked, "What are we going to do with that?"

I looked at the little bottle and said, "I got it. C'mon."

We went on the back deck and opened the bottle. We threw it all overboard. We put the gold back where it belonged—in the bay. I took Eric to the airport in Ketchikan and a friend of mine, Fred Weiler[30], flew up to help me bring the boat home.

---

[30] At the end of Chapter 3: Hunting is a picture of Fred with Ken elk hunting in Halfway.

Chapter 48: Trouble at Sportcraft

IN ADDITION to high water at Sportcraft, we occasionally had to deal with high tempers. One summer there was a gas shortage at the moorage. I was working inside. Dad was outside at the gas pump and having some trouble with the customers who wanted more gas than we were allowed to sell. One of the boats had two young couples in it. I came out of the shop and heard them giving Dad a bad time. It pissed me off. I told them to get the hell out of there—they weren't getting any gas.

It wasn't smart to challenge these guys in front of their girlfriends. They maneuvered the boat to the dock and one guy jumped out. He was going to whup me. It was not going to be a pretty scene if I beat this guy up in front of the customers. As he came toward me, I rushed in and grabbed him by the waist and, while he was trying to hit me, I jumped into the river and took him to the bottom. The water was only ten feet deep, but deep enough that he forgot about fighting. I let him go and he went to the surface, grabbed the rail, and started to pull himself up onto the dock.

If I let him get out of the water ahead of me, I was going to be in trouble. I got behind and put him in a choke hold while I levered my feet on his hips.

Now I had his attention.

I whispered into his ear, "If you fight, we'll go back to the bottom of the river. If you get out of the water, and get in your boat without saying a thing, you can go." He thought about it for a while, but finally conceded.

Before I let him go, I said, "Now you know, if you say anything, I'm taking you back to the bottom of the river. Okay?"

"Okay." He got out and left.

No blood, no more trouble, and Dad continued to pump gas.

One night two guys got onto one of the docks with covered slips and were burglarizing boats. Eric heard them and called me. He and his wife, Kim, were living in their float home at one end of the moorage, and Kathy and I were living in our float home at the other end. Eric had his pistol in his back pocket and I had my pistol in my back pocket. We went down to the docks, captured the two guys, and put them under citizen arrest. We called the police and they were going to come and get them.

While we waited for the police, the guys had a chance to think and one of them thought he was going to take me on. I got him down on the dock—I was on the bottom with my arms around him and he was facing upward. I had to be careful—the dock was only a couple feet wide and I couldn't roll either way or I would go in the river.

Eric didn't know what was going on. He pulled out his gun and put it in the guy's chest.

"Hold it Eric, I've got him," I told him. I knew if he shot it was going to go through me, too.

When the police came, both guys went quietly.

Eric and I had another adventure—this one involved saving a woman's life. It was a weekend night and Kathy and I were in our float home watching TV. We heard a loud commotion on the bank and ran out to see what was going on. There wasn't anything unusual on the docks, but a man on the shore was pointing into the water and yelling, "My girlfriend, my girlfriend!"

Kathy and I looked down and saw headlights shining under the dock.

By this time, Eric had joined us. I told him, "You dive on the passenger side and I'll dive down on the driver's side. Try to open the door. I'll do the same. There's a woman in there and we've got to get her out."

When I got to the driver's side window, I could see the woman behind the wheel, but the door was jammed and I couldn't open it.

We surfaced and I asked Eric if he could open the other door.

"Yeah."

"OK, you've got to go in and pull her out."

When he resurfaced his face was as white as a ghost and his eyes were huge.

"Well, did you get her out?" I asked.

"I pulled on her leg and it came off!"

"Well, go down and pull on her other leg."

We got the woman to shore and placed her on the bank. She didn't seem to be breathing. I had Eric start chest compression. I tilted back her head and opened her mouth to start mouth-to-mouth resuscitation. Her mouth was a filthy mess of rotten teeth and she reeked of alcohol. I yelled for Kathy, who was still standing on the dock. After all, I figured, she's a nurse and this was her job.

It would take too long for her to run down the dock, up the ramp, and over to where we had the woman on the bank. Kathy didn't hesitate—she dove into the water, swam over to us, and got the woman breathing again.

We rescued the woman and her leg.

Now, I don't expect gratitude for doing things like this. When they showed up, I told the newspaper reporters I didn't know anything about it, and sent them to talk to Eric and Kathy. Shows of gratitude make me a little uncomfortable, but not as much as getting sued for helping someone.

The woman's car had been parked in the lot above the moorage. The lot is owned by the City and we lease it from them. Instead of putting the car in Reverse, she put it in Drive and drove over a small dirt barrier, down the bank, and under one of our docks.

I guess she thought we were supposed to protect drunks from using the wrong gear. She sued us and the City. When the City talked to us about it, Kathy told them, in no uncertain terms, to not pay her. We didn't give her any money, but the City gave her a settlement. It infuriated Kathy, but I figure it's just the way people are and some people can't be helped.

But it did seem funny that the same City that would pay off a drunk whose life we'd saved would try to put Sportcraft out of business.

Chapter 49: Fighting City Hall

WHEN I originally stood on the banks of the Willamette River in 1969 and pictured a resource that would provide access to the river for a lot of people, I gave up building apartments—a lucrative business—to go into the marina business on the Willamette River, which has not been at all profitable. I didn't expect it to be like developing properties; my main goal was to help people get access to the river.

In the beginning, we had a good working relationship with the City. Then things deteriorated.

Today, it's disappointing to see where my and my family's efforts have ended up. In March 2013 there were a dozen boats on the river where there used to be hundreds. Instead of boats and salmon, the river is full of sea lions, and this is over a hundred miles upstream from saltwater. We have had up to twenty huge sea lions on the dock in front of Kathy's house, the dock where fishing boats used to moor. Eric has pictures of

Sea lions making themselves at home in front of Kathy's house at Sportcraft Landing (2013)

fishermen holding up their catch of steelhead—the line, the hook, and the head of the fish—nothing else. Instead of hunting for themselves, the sea lions have learned to follow boats and eat the fish hooked by fishermen.

Besides the expense of building and maintaining Sportcraft Landing, I continually fight the City of Oregon City to stay in business. In 2012 I presented a letter to the City describing Sportcraft's history and the issues we faced.

History of Sportcraft Landing, By Ken Dye

I purchased Sportcraft Landing from the Huff family, Clair and Ruth in 1969. I met them while diving for sunken logs in the Willamette River in 1962. I became well acquainted with them during the flood of 1964. At that time, Sportcraft was just a few log docks and a 2x12 board nailed to the length of a log for a ramp from shore to the first floating dock. Clair had an old G.I. Boom truck that was used to set the log in place and adjust as the water changed elevation.

Clair and his son, Barry, had pumped out the old wood Boones Ferry Barge near Wilsonville and towed it to Sportcraft Landing. They built a building on it that became the Tackle Shop and Snack Shop. The dock upstream from the Tackle Shop was the gas dock with a fuel tank and gas pump. The moorage also had a small float home where the Huffs lived with about 200 ft. of log dock for tying fishing boats to. All this hung off a log dolphin. During the winter, this floating equipment was taken to the river's shore and fastened to the cottonwood trees until Spring Salmon Season and Summer Season. When I purchased the moorage equipment in 1969, I envisioned it as a much more functional facility permanently attached to steel piling with much better equipment.

Prior to my purchase, the I-205 Bridge was being built. During this period, the moorage was almost lost. The plans for the Bridge Development did not include access to the moorage. Ruth Huff organized the fishermen and encouraged them to write the Governor, Tom McCall. He became involved and had things redesigned to include an access road under the bridge. Had it not been for Ruth, the moorage would have been lost. After this event, Crown Zellerbach, who owned the land upstream from the bridge, donated the land to the City for parking and boat ramp. Later, I purchased a 450 ft. strip of land from Crown Zellerbach so I could lease the offshore property in front of the City Parking Lot. I went to the City Manager and explained my vision to create a substantial moorage operation. They thought it was a great idea and encouraged me to continue. The City and I worked together like partners. Anytime there was a problem, I went to the City Manager, Al Simonson, and we would work our way through it. The City at this time developed the parking lot and the boat ramp. I filled the area upstream from the parking lot, which created a shelf that I rocked and black topped. This area fronts my strip of land and my upper offshore lease, and creates additional parking.

I then installed a number of steel pilings, new docks with fingers to moor boats to, built a proper and safe access ramp, a large sales building, new fuel dock with fuel tank on land with proper plumbing and electrical system, sewer system hooked to City sewer, added four each covered moorage buildings, and added more Sales and Service to supplement income from slip rent.

After approximately ten years, it became apparent this project was not going to be profitable! We sold the Sales and Service part of the business to Larry Bigbee and named it Sportcraft Marina, a separate business entity of Sportcraft Landing. He leased our Sales and Service building and related equipment on a percentage of gross sales. By using the shelf area of land I built upstream of our parking area for storage of boats and trailers, Larry was able to build a Sales and Service business that created several permanent and seasonal jobs.

I knew I could never retire from this non-profitable business, so I leased 1500 ft. of river frontage on the Multnomah Channel near Scappoose, Oregon. I then built Scappoose Moorage, Ltd. and Channel Moorage, Inc. This is where I currently live and work.

These moorage businesses, Sportcraft Landing, Scappoose Moorage, and Channel Moorage are all possible because of my profession as a Professional Diver. I did heavy marine salvage for ten years, covering an area from the Arctic Ocean to South America. I also owned two other diving businesses, all profitable ventures. I was involved in the diving business from the age of 20 to 60. This allowed me to earn more than a living, thus I was able to invest in these moorages. Sportcraft Landing cost me about $1,000,000 and I'm still investing in it. Several years ago, I sold Sportcraft to my son, Eric Dye. He has built a floating home and now lives at Sportcraft. He operates a dock building and installation business from Sportcraft Landing. About the time I sold to Eric, our lease with the City ran out. Larry was forced to give up our lease and build a building on McLoughlin Blvd. near Milwaukie.

This has cost us 50% of our income. The City would not allow us to continue using the portion of the upstream parking lot for boat and trailer storage. The City has refused to renew our lease for a number of years. Finally, we received a short term lease, but the damage was done. Without the Sales and Service income, Eric could not afford to maintain or upgrade the facilities. Last year, he built a four-bay boat house for the Clackamas County Sheriff Department. Last winter, I installed $70,000 worth of high quality steel docks around this building to tie the boat house building to ensure its safety and long-term dock system. I will never see this money or gain any return from it!

Let's summarize this story: The Dye Family has made huge donations to the boating public of Oregon City. I'm now 73 years old and I need to quit doing things that are not going to give me and my family a return on its investment.

There are three possible solutions to this problem:

1) The City needs to recognize the damage it's done to this business and the boating public. Forgive all leases and fees, the State Land Board must also forgive all offshore lease fees. This business is non-profitable and should be treated as one.

This would give the Dye family a chance to upgrade and operate the Sales and Services in hopes of breaking even financially and continue to operate the Marina for the public.

2) The City could buy us out and let tax payers take the losses.

3) The City can re-connect with the Dye Family and work with us, not against us. We would continue our donation to the boating public.

I would like to explain why it's so expensive to operate a moorage at this location. The 1964 flood was 49 feet high with a very fast current. Many people don't remember or know what impact this had on the river and moorage   The steel piling must reach to an elevation of 52 feet.   The outer piling must be three pilings in a group creating what we call a dolphin.   The pilings must be welded together at the top, with hardware connecting the piling to the docks and must be extremely strong to endure the potentially strong currents from high waters and floods.

After the 1996 flood, at an elevation of 46 feet, we lost a number of pilings. They bent over with the current.   We replaced them with a new steel piling, and not only welded the tops together, but we installed steel cables from the top of each dolphin through the moorage, tying them all together.   Then the cables went to a specially designed dolphin at the upper end of the moorage.   These dolphins are next to the shore and are designed to take a lot of tons of pressure.   These are our anchors, and if one goes—they all go.   In all my travels of the West Coast of this continent, I have never seen a moorage supported like this.   It isn't necessary except at Oregon City, Sportcraft Landing, due to the rising river.   This is a very unique and special situation for a Marina.

Let me explain what 49 feet of water means.   This 49 foot of water goes over McLoughlin Blvd. and floods all the stores at the Oregon City Shopping Center. During the '64 flood, a friend of mine caught a steelhead trying to get over a road divider on McLoughlin Blvd. at the Shopping Center.   These floods aren't going to quit coming.   Whoever operates this moorage must be ready for the worst flood every year and understand what to do to save the equipment, docks, buildings and boats. This extreme flood only comes every 15-30 years, but you have to be ready for it every year, or the river wins.

The reader of this report should go to Sportcraft Landing and walk down the ramp to the docks.   Check out the piling and support system here; batter piling, connector between dock and piling, and the elevation of the piling.   Imagine water to within three feet of the top piling and a very fast and dangerous flowing river.   You will then get some idea of what I'm trying to explain.

Please, City of Oregon City, join us as it was in 1969, a partnership with the Dye Family so we can continue to provide access for thousands of people to the river.

The City never made a formal announcement, but now (2013) they are working with us better again.   It seems that everything between the City and Sportcraft is peaceful again.

Chapter 50: Scappoose Moorage & Channel Moorage

AFTER BUILDING and running Sportcraft Landing at Oregon City for ten years, I realized I wouldn't be able to retire with having only this single marina.

I liked the moorage business, but realized it's a little short on the profit side. I looked around the area for a location that didn't have such radical conditions as Oregon City with its 49-foot water levels and heavy currents. The Multnomah Channel, a twenty-one mile long offshoot of the Willamette River that empties into the Columbia River, seemed like a good area. I had a friend that owned a moorage and sales business in Scappoose, Oregon, about halfway down the Channel. I contacted him and he introduced me to a farmer, Fred Bernet, who lived downstream from his business. At our first meeting, Fred and I were talking terms and made a deal for 865 feet of frontage plus options on another 400 feet.

I started building Scappoose Boat Moorage in 1980. Connie and Larry from the foam business were silent partners. (Both men died a few years ago and I continued to pay a portion of the profits to the widows until recently when I offered to buy out the widows and will eventually own Scappoose Moorage directly.) From another landowner I leased 100 feet upstream from the 865 foot piece and began building docks. Some of the docks were covered slips. When I finished the 965 feet of Scappoose Moorage in 2002, I picked up the option on the next 400 feet from Fred, which became Channel Moorage, Inc. I built this moorage without any partners and treat it as a separate business.

In 2005 I finished both moorages. Today about 200 boats are moored here, about half of them are under cover. There is a repair yard, two access ramps, and two utility buildings. The moorages are connected at the main dock, but each has its own parking lot, mailboxes, restrooms with showers, and laundry facilities. There are a wood shop and storage lockers on the main dock, and garages in one of the parking lots. The manager's home and office is at the upstream end and I have a townhouse apartment at the other end. My grandson, Matt, is in charge of maintenance and lives in a small combination boat house/float home near the manager's office. Most of the docks are steel and concrete; some are log and plank with foam flotation. We still have a few log docks and timber frame covered slips.

The reason I could build these moorages is due to the profit I made as a professional diver, particularly installing foam under floating buildings and docks. The two moorages provide me with my income.

Chapter 51: Disaster Strikes

THE SAME year I started building Scappoose Moorage my son Eric turned sixteen and wanted a car. We sold him my wife Kathy's old Pontiac. I told him that he had to drive responsibly or I'd take the car away. When he got his first ticket for speeding, we had a pretty heavy-duty discussion and I warned him, "One more ticket and I'm taking the car away."

I was divorced from his mother and didn't have custody of him, but I had a lot of authority. My friend Dean, the deputy sheriff on the river for Clackamas County, had married my ex-wife, Sandy. We were all friends; there was never any problems there. Sometimes I had the kids, sometimes she had the kids. We shared them well.

Eric got a second speeding ticket. Sandy and Dean decided they weren't going to tell me because they knew I'd take the car away. They kept it a secret.

Eric came up for a hearing on his ticket. Dean found a flaw in the ticket; I don't know what it was. Eric went to the courthouse with two of his buddies, who were brothers, and the boys' father, Butch, a customer of mine at Sportcraft Landing.

Eric beat the ticket.

I was at Sportcraft working on the *Que Sera* when Butch came down to the moorage.

"Did you hear about Eric beating his ticket?" Butch asked.

"I didn't know Eric had gotten a ticket," I replied.

"I didn't think so," he said.

He explained how it was for speeding and how he beat it. While Butch was still talking, the voice came to me and said, "If you don't act responsibly, there's going to be a disaster with that car."

I asked Butch, "Do you know where Eric is right now?"

He said Eric was with his two sons, but that they were all coming down to the moorage later. The boys planned to go to Butch's boat first. I asked him to tell Eric that I was working on my boat and to come down to see me when he got there. I told him not to let him know that I knew about the ticket.

Eric never showed. I knew I had to do something, but wasn't sure exactly what. I didn't act fast enough, there was an accident, and someone was killed.

After a while, when I figured Eric had recovered somewhat, I talked to him about the accident. He came to me and asked me, "Do you think I was responsible for the accident?"

It was a hard question and I had to be careful not to place too much or too little blame.

"Well, you are half responsible," I told him.

"How?"

"Well, you failed to check the road ahead of you. The other person wasn't acting responsibly either. He had half of the responsibility. You both broke the rules and the two broken rules are what caused the accident."

We put the car in the backyard with the boats. It was awhile before Eric drove again.

After the message about the car, I didn't receive any more messages. A number of years went by and I was pretty concerned. That was the only time I had not obeyed the voice. I had tried, but I hadn't tried hard enough. It bothered me. I felt I was out of favor. Finally, through prayer, I asked for confirmation: *If I am out of favor, I need to know. I screwed up. I accept that. If I'm not out of favor, I need to know that, too. Anything. Just let me know.*

I asked for help and tried to put that problem to rest.

Chapter 52: Halfway

WHEN I bought Sportcraft Landing from the Huff' in 1969 they invited me to come to Halfway, Oregon, where Clair Huff's father lived, and where they were born and raised. They thought I might like the hunting and fishing.

That first year I couldn't make it.

In 1970 I had a diving job during deer season and couldn't make it, but by elk season I was available, so I took the dive gear out of my van and put in hunting equipment. I left Oregon City early in the morning and hunted pheasants in LaGrande for a couple of hours. Then I headed to Baker City, where I turned east on the road heading to Halfway. I stopped in Richland, hunted some more pheasants, and about 3:30 went over the hill to Halfway.

Going down into Pine Valley, I saw the town of Halfway for the first time. The population was only about 150 then. I could see the Cornucopia Mountains up the valley from town. I admired the pretty valley with the small town in it. The lower end was spread with sage brush covered hills, and the upper end was timber with large mountains beyond. There were expanses of ranchland with cattle around the valley.

As I was looking down on the valley, I got a spiritual message. Not a voice message, but a knowledge message, which said to me, *You've found home.*

It kind of startled me and I said to myself, *I'm not looking for a home.* But when I repeated the words to myself—*You've found home*—I felt very good. What was going on? What was this good feeling when I repeated the words? The spiritual side was busy doing their thing.

I hunted with Clair that first season and we discussed my bringing my then-wife Sandy and the kids up the next summer to fish the creeks, the Snake River impoundments, and Hells Canyon. Not a bad setting for a family outing!

I took my family to Halfway every summer to go fishing. We would take materials to do repair jobs to Clair's father's house that we stayed in. I worked on the house, built a patio, repaired the roof, and remodeled inside. We were trading repair work for house privileges.

Later, my second wife Kathy helped me with these projects.

When I first invited Kathy to come to Halfway with me, I called Ruth and said, "I'm bringing a friend with me."

"Okay, he can have the other guest room."

"No, it's a woman friend and she's going to sleep with me."

Poor Ruth. Sandy and I had just divorced and I don't think she expected this. When we arrived, Clair went straight to Kathy and gave her a big hug. From then on, she adored him. We all had a wonderful weekend.

Each fall I would go to Halfway for deer and elk season. It was great fun with Ruth and Clair; they were two wonderful people.

Ruth and Clair used to love to go to Mexico. As they got older, they would go to San Diego to Ruth's sister's house instead. One year they had to come home early. Kathy and I were in California visiting relatives when we heard Clair's cancer had progressed. We came back early and went to the hospital to see him. He was so drugged up he couldn't even visit. We took Ruth home later, with plans to go back the next day. Kathy told me she couldn't go— she couldn't stand to see Clair that way.

The next morning, when I took Ruth to the hospital, she said to me, "Kenny, why don't you go up and see Clair and I'll go to the cafeteria to get something to eat. I haven't had breakfast."

I was expecting to see him comatose like the day before. But there was Clair— up and alert. We spent the next three hours talking about hunting, etc. That night he died. I still think of those few hours with Clair as a blessing.

It's not unusual for people to rally just before they die.

In the 1920s, my dad's sister, Alma, and her husband bought a nice little house in the middle of the oilfields in Huntington Beach, California. They didn't have any kids and saved all their money.

Years later, I was selling concrete docks[31] in California when the cousins asked me to be sure Aunt Alma had a proper will drawn up and asked me to be the executor.

Aunt Zelpha, Uncle Blackie's wife and I were extremely close; we had a relationship similar to the one between my mom and me. Their oldest daughter, Rhonda, was to be co-executor.

The only way I knew to help Aunt Alma was to set up a trust and I explained it to her in detail; Alma wasn't very worldly and kept large sums in her checking account. I asked her pertinent questions and she told me what she wanted to do with her assets. Aunt Alma had six nieces and nephews. We addressed the money first.

"I want all six of you to divide it up," she instructed.

"What do you want to do with the house?" I asked.

She started telling me a story: "I've been thinking about this a lot. I want you, Deanne, and Norman to have the house. (My brother) Blackie has a nice house and his daughters Rhonda and Zanna are going to get that. My sister Ruby has a nice house," Alma continued, "and her daughter, Carol, is going to get that. Your parents didn't have a house to leave you kids, so I want you kids to have my house."

My parents had sold the pale yellow house in Ashland and never had much equity in it.

I wrote down her desire to leave the house to us, but didn't think it was proper to include why. If I had, perhaps it would have saved hard feelings with the rest of the family later. It just didn't occur to me that you could put that kind of detail in a will.

I was living in Oregon when Aunt Alma got cancer.

My cousin Rhonda called, "Ken, you gotta get down here quick. Aunt Alma is failing."

---

[31] I was introduced to the concrete dock building business just out of high school when I worked for Croft & Neville. When I was building Scappoose Moorage I looked at the market and saw that concrete docks were becoming popular, but I didn't like the standard docks I saw. They were small sections held together with heavy timbers on the side, proving a concrete walking surface but the concrete was not part of the structure. The movement of the water eventually made the timbers loose. It was a never-ending project to keep them tight. I wanted to see if we could make a long, continuous pour where the sides were trusses. Sig, a guy I'd originally hired as a kid to work at the moorage, and I started playing with that idea and saw that we could do it. I put a few of the new docks into Channel Moorage. It made a wonderful dock and I patented the process. The problem with building docks on land is the time concrete takes to cure and the logistics of moving large, completed docks to the water so I built a dry dock and built the docks in the water. Now we didn't have to use a crane to move the docks. Plus, concrete cures better in water—it doesn't dry out as fast. However, it was going to take too much capital and time to set up production to compete in the market so I sold the business and the patent to a concrete company in Wilsonville and Sig went to work for them. I learned you can make a good dock out of steel and it's more versatile and that's what I use today.

When I arrived in Huntington Beach, Alma was full of tubes and comatose like Clair had been. While Alma was alert, Rhonda had been bringing her mail to the nursing home. Alma's checkbook and bills were by the side of her bed. She had $500,000 cash in the bank. To help with taxes, we had to get rid of some of it before she died. Each heir could get $10,000 tax free. Alma was not dead yet, but she was dying. We needed two doctor's signatures on a document stipulating she was incapacitated so we could write the checks. Rhonda and I chased down the doctors. We were filling out checks in the car and getting them in the mail. They had to be postmarked before she died. It took all day. With a sigh of relief, we did it.

We were driving by the nursing home and stopped to see Alma. Rhonda went in ahead of me. When I got to the room, Alma was sitting on the bed with her checkbook in her lap.

"What's this with my checkbook?" she demanded to know.

Fortunately, Rhonda could think faster on her feet than I could and told her, "Alma, I had to pay a bunch of your utility bills. That's why the checks are missing."

Afterwards Rhonda was frantic. "Ken, what are we going to do? How do we explain what we've done?"

"Don't worry, she's going to die tonight," I reassured her. And she did.

We sold the house for $600,000. I don't know if the house was the reason, but after Alma died things changed between me and the family. I had the boat in Anacortes where my dad's brother Blackie and his wife Zelpha's youngest daughter, Zanna, lived. Uncle Blackie had died by this time. Zanna brought her mom to the boat. I sat next to Aunt Zelpha. I'd always been close to Zelpha and now she wouldn't talk to me. I'd ask her a question and she'd answer it curtly. Today, Norm has contact with our cousin, Rhonda, and her husband, Tom, but I was so disappointed—I'd done everything right, what Alma wanted, I didn't influence her at all—that I haven't talked to any of the cousins since.

When Clair Huff got cancer and died, Ruth was near 80 years old. Kathy and I discussed buying a house of our own in Halfway. We knew when Ruth passed on we were going to lose our house privileges. We started looking at properties the next summer. The local realtor took us to several houses. We made offers on two houses that we felt we could fix up for our needs. We reduced the asking price a ccuple thousand dollars. Both owners were upset with our offers and rejected them.

The following spring I went to Halfway and got in touch with the realtor to see what was going on in the local housing market. She indicated there weren't any homes for sale in Halfway at that time. I asked her about the two homes we made offers on the previous summer. She laughed and said, "They both sold last fall."

I asked her what they sold for and she said for less than I had offered! What's going on? Without thinking, I asked her if there was any property outside of town that was buildable. She thought for a moment, then answered, "Yes, but it's very rough property and would be expensive to build on".

I suggested we go look at it. It was ranch land a mile-and-a-half up the valley from town on Pine Creek. There were two five-acre parcels. A house had been built on the first five acres by a couple from California. Another couple bought the second five acres, but hadn't built on it. Now they were ready to get their money back. The realtor couldn't walk through the area because it was so overgrown with brush and trees. She explained where the corners of the property were located. I climbed over the fence to a pile of brush in the middle of the plot and got high enough to see one corner post. I could get to the other corner by following the creek so was able to get a pretty good picture of the land. It also had a secondary creek cutting through the middle of the five acres.

Cabin under construction at Halfway, Oregon (est. 1987)

I returned to my truck where the realtor was waiting. I was sure she was thinking I'd seen enough. I asked her what the owners were asking and she got upset and tried talking me out of offering anything. By then we knew each other fairly well and she wanted to protect me from making a mistake. She said the owners were asking $12,000. I told her to offer $11,500 and again she tried to discourage me. I insisted, and they accepted the offer.

Now the work began! This all took place back in 1984.

I built a road to the middle of the five acres, which wound around a swampy area and crossed the creek to the building site I had chosen. I filled in the swamp at the upper end and put a bridge over the small creek, which had to be strong enough to handle concrete trucks. We brought in a trailer house first. After I built a shed for tools next to our trailer, we brought my parents' fifth wheel trailer for my brother Norm to use. We had to build roofs over the trailers before winter hit with heavy snow.

Over the next thirty years I built our log home. Besides the two-story, two-bedroom cabin, we put in a sand filter sewer system, cleared and planted grass, put in a well, brought in an electrical system, a propane fuel tank, gas and diesel storage, a large pond in way of the swamp area, planted an orchard, and built a large barn with a bunkhouse, and a shed for a tractor and attachments.

A couple of years ago (2011), I stood in the middle of this project and thought, *I've just completed a survival home.* It has everything you need to survive. Besides all the modern conveniences, it has a woodstove for heat, an old wood range that can be cooked on, a bunkhouse in the barn with a woodstove, two large diesel generators, and an electric heat pump and a large propane tank for when times are good. When I purchased the place, I never thought of it as a survival home. It just turned out that way.

It is also a family gathering place. I have plans to acquire the house and land next door and turn the two properties into a park-like setting for the family to enjoy.

The cabin at Halfway, Oregon (est. 1992)

Kathy and I spent a week there last July. We were sitting on the side deck having our evening drink. I explained to her the project was done after thirty years, with no specific plan as to its purpose.

"What would you change and do different?" I asked her.

She thought then answered, "Not a thing."

I explained that's how I felt, too. No planning, just doing. What's going on? It had turned out just the way we wanted. Was the spiritual working through me to get this end result?

Chapter 53: *Que Sera II*

IN 2005 I finished building Scappoose and Channel Moorages. For some unknown reason, I decided to build a trawler style boat. I still had the first *Que Sera* sailboat that I salvaged from the sand and rebuilt. Now I had this notion of building a 60-foot trawler. I designed the hull as a rough-sea boat that would ride heavy seas, not fight them—similar to my motor sailboat, but in a trawler style. This boat would have a large house and be more comfortable than a sailboat.

I hired a marine architect to do the prints and started building the hull in my work yard where I build docks. I knew I was in for a big job. One day I stood back and looked at what I had started. I gave it some serious thought, *What the hell am I doing? I don't need another boat. I'm not going anywhere. I've done that. This is going to be time consuming and expensive and I'm 66 years old!*

I put $460,000 plus my labor for four years into building the *Que Sera II.* With the expense of the yard, tools, and equipment I would need to sell it for $700,000 to break even. But I enjoyed every bit of the experience.

As long as I was building a wheel for myself, I thought it would be neat for friends who were building or rebuilding their boats to have wheels made from a black walnut tree I'd salvaged when working on the first *Que Sera*—I used the fiddle-back-grained wood on the interiors of both my boats. I talked one of our marina customers, Jerry, a retired high school shop teacher, into shaping the spokes and wheel sections. Jerry was depressed from a recent prostrate surgery and it seemed like this project would do him some good and I think it did—by the middle of the first day he was proudly showing others what he was doing and explaining how to make a ship's wheel.

Dick Long (seen in picture sitting on Ken's leg while suiting up to dive on the *Brother Jonathan*) told me black walnut was "Jonah wood"—that it is bad luck to put black walnut on a boat,[32] but I think it looks great.

After the *Que Sera II* was in the water, I determined it was unstable. I had not ballasted it yet, so I took the boat to Astoria to build a shoe on the keel, about four-inches deep by eight-inches wide, and filled it with lead. We launched the boat again, but it still was not stable, so we hauled it out again. I then built another four-inch by eight-inch shoe, filled it with lead, and welded it to the extension we had just finished. Now we had an extension of the keel of eight-inches by eight-inches with 14,000 pounds of lead. When we launched again, the boat was stable.

This boat will cross heavy seas safely. It has a very efficient hull. I spent a lot of money and had a lot of fun building it, but couldn't help but think, *Why did I do it? I'm not going anywhere! I wonder if my spiritual friends are having some fun with me?* I didn't start out to build a survival home, but I did. I also built two survival boats. All these projects just felt right. I still don't know why I have two boats that will cross an ocean or why I built a survival home; it just seemed the right thing to do.

Que Sera II nearing completion in the work yard at Channel Moorage, Scappoose, Oregon (est. 2006)

---

[32] From: "Folklore and the Sea", by Horace Beck – ISBN: 0-7858-1119-2   An old waterman once bought a very handsome skiff there for five dollars. From the day he bought it he had nothing but trouble. It sank, broke loose, was stolen, leaked; and whenever he went out in it, things went wrong. He caught no fish, lost oars, a storm came up. Finally he decided to repaint it and stripped off some of the paint. The skiff was made of black walnut! He did the only thing he could do--sold it to a tourist. ... Just as a dog with a bad name gains the reputation of being a sheep killer, so does the black walnut become the scapegoat for every miserable boatbuilder and lubberly sailor in the area.

Chapter 54: We Can Communicate With You in Many Ways

FOR TWENTY-THREE years I did not receive a voice message, not since 1980 when Eric was 16 and there was the accident. It was hard. It is easy to become addicted to the voice, to count on something outside of yourself to make decisions for you. I knew this and knew I had to figure things out for myself, that I couldn't—and shouldn't—depend on the voice to live my life, but I missed it and wanted to know why I was no longer receiving messages. I was afraid I was out of favor for not having responded quickly enough to the last message and someone died.

Then a couple of things happened to make me rethink how I received messages. The first was during deer hunting season. I took Kathy, a friend, Bob Matson, and our kids up to the cabin in Halfway to go hunting. It was a wet deer season. Kathy had gotten a tag for the Keating District and I'd gotten a tag for the Pine District. Our cabin sits on the border line between the two districts. I told Kathy I'd take her out on opening day on her hunt and, after she got her deer, I'd go over to the other district for my deer.

We drove the pickup up to a place we knew from prior years. As we neared the top of the ridge we came around a little corner, and I got the very, very strong premonition that there was a nice buck up this ridge. Without thinking about it, I told Kathy, "Why don't I stop here and you can walk up the ridge. There's a nice buck up that ridge."

Because of the rain and the cold, she didn't want to go. We went to the end of the road and turned the truck to go back down the hill. By now it had started to snow. As we approached the ridge in the truck, I got the strong premonition again, *There is a nice, big buck up that ridge.*

I stopped the truck and said, "Kathy, you need to walk up that ridge. There's a nice buck up there."

She still didn't want to go and suggested that I walk up the ridge. I took her gun, walked up about a hundred yards, and killed a very nice four-point buck.

I hadn't seen it, but somehow I knew it was there. Later I asked Kathy why she didn't think it was odd that I knew the buck was there. She said, "Oh, Ken, you're always doing things like that."

The next day I went out with Bob. After several days of hunting Bob still hadn't gotten his buck. The following Wednesday, I took Bob out again. First we talked about where we should go. I said, "Let's go out to the grass hills." We had never hunted there for deer. As we were driving I said, "There's a big buck on top of the high hill that has the power lines on it." Again, I had no idea how I knew this, I just knew and spoke without thinking. We tried for hours to go up the road on the backside, but the truck got stuck in the mud. We were running low on gas and it was raining again. It was a mess. We came back down the hill and went to town for gas. We pulled out of the gas station and I turned back toward the hill.

"Aren't we going back to the cabin?" Bob asked.

"No. We've got to go out and get that big buck on the top of the hill," I said.

We went up the other side of the hill and managed to make it that way. We pulled up on the very top of the hill. I pulled the truck off to the side and turned off the engine. I started scoping the ridges and spotted a doe five or six hundred yards below us. The grass was fairly high and as I looked down past her, I saw big horns sticking out of the grass.

I told Bob, "There he is." We had found him.

Bob got him. As we were taking the buck out, Bob said, "Ken, you've known that deer was there all day. How'd you know that?"

"I don't know," I told him. "I just knew." In both cases, I had no pre-thought before I spoke; the words came out my mouth without me thinking about what I was saying.

The next winter, I took my friend Richard Whited (the schoolmate who as a boy had gotten an illness that left him permanently fidgety—hunting was one thing he could still enjoy), to Halfway to go coyote hunting. We were driving along the Powder River. We always put the guns up front in the cab when driving canyons where we know there to be coyote. We came around a corner and saw a draw coming from the left side below us, but we couldn't see up the draw.

I told Dick, "That next draw has a coyote in it." We hadn't seen a coyote until then, but I somehow knew one was there.

As we pulled down the draw, I looked over my left shoulder back up the draw and sure enough, there was a coyote over on the hillside. I got him.

Dick asked, "How'd you know that coyote was there? You couldn't see up that draw."

I said, "I don't know, Dick, I just knew."

Another time shortly after that I was working at the moorage in Scappoose. It was about eight o'clock in the morning and I decided to drive to town to get some parts at the hardware store. I always scoped out the fields when I went to town. Being a hunter, I got into that habit, but for years I'd never seen a coyote there.

When I came out of the hardware store I went to grab the handle on the door of the pickup truck and it hit me hard that I would see a coyote on the way home. It wasn't the voice, just a strong premonition.

On the drive home, I was looking every place. The feeling had been so strong. Sure enough, there was a coyote out in the field. I drove by and went down to the moorage and said to my friend Richard (the same Richard I saw the coyote with in Halfway) "Get your gun. There's a coyote down the road." We went back and got it.

Afterwards, I sat in my truck thinking about this and the three previous incidents where I knew an animal was there, but I couldn't have known it on my own. It dawned on me what was going on. I was not out of favor. I couldn't see those animals. They weren't in view, but I was told they were there. When I made this realization, I started laughing, wondering how I could have been so dense that it took four examples to get it through my head, and said, "Thank you. I appreciate it. I got the message and I'm okay now."

The voice answered, "We can communicate with you in many ways."

It was clear to me that all along the spiritual had been there, guiding me. That they had and could use me as a puppet to help others. By making me know and say things when I could not have any personal knowledge, the spirit world was reminding me it could take over my mind and my body and my voice.

Then I knew they had always been there.

Part 7: What does it mean?

Chapter 55: A Recap of the Messages

Voice Messages:

1948   9 years old: "You are going to be a professional diver."

1956 Summer 17 years old: "She's pregnant."

1958   19 years old: "You are going to work here" (Croft & Neville)

Date unknown: Question of shooting deer beyond my ability: "What did you do with the meat?"

Date unknown: What can I do to show my appreciation? "People"

1975   35 years old: "You are going to raise these boys. You can't trust that responsibility to another man."

1980   40 or 41 years old: "If you don't act responsibly, there is going to be a disaster with that car."

2002 or 03 63 or 64 years old: "We can communicate with you in many ways."

Other messages:

1969 Vision of the tunnel with a blockage ahead

1970 When driving into valley near Halfway for the first time, the knowledge message: "You've found Home."

Things I said without conscious thought of how I knew the information (age 63 or 64). Through me to Kathy: "There's a large buck up that ridge.

Through me to Bob: "There's a large buck on top of that hill."

Through me to Dick: "There's a coyote in the next draw."

To Self: "There's a coyote on the way home."

THE FIRST time I heard the voice was when I was nine years old and was told, "You are going to be a professional diver." The voice provided the direction. I had to do the work. As a result, I was always successful, both as a salvage diver and, later, in the foam business. With two partners I salvaged over two million board feet of lumber from the bottoms of lakes and rivers that had been lost for decades. With no professional training I salvaged difficult wrecks from the Arctic Ocean to Mexico—without any failures and no serious injuries to myself or our crews. I invented a new system for installing foam flotation that was faster and more accurate than any other method. As a result of these ventures I gained financial independence and was able to build three moorages that provide access to the river for many people as well as provide an income for me and my family. I could not have done this alone.

The second time I heard the voice was the summer I was seventeen and dating Sandy and was told, "She's pregnant." We were able to get married in time so that Sandy's mother never knew. We had three great kids together.

A couple of years later I was told I would work for Croft & Neville. This gave me the opportunity to do three professional dives. I also learned about the dock business, which I was able to use later when I designed and patented my own concrete dock system. The manager of Croft & Neville, like the managers later at Medco and Crown Zellerbach, had never heard of me or asked about my credentials. All of them hired me on faith. I believe I was led to these businesses and to Fred Devine Diving and Salvage.

I was thirty-four when the voice told me I would raise Kathy's boys. We were married a year later. I love her and the boys grew into wonderful men.

Five years later I was warned that there would be a disaster with my son's car. It was the only time I didn't respond fast enough and a disaster occurred.

In between those years I was hunting and wondering to myself why it seemed so easy for me to hit the mark—I knew the shots I made, starting when I was twelve, were not humanly possible. I was repeatedly led to the spot where the deer was resting, hidden from view. When I asked for an explanation, the voice responded, "What did you do with the meat?" Of course: I had fed a lot of people who may not have had meat in the house any other way.

When I asked how I could show my appreciation for the benefits the spiritual world had given me, they said, "People." I had to find the answer to that message. To me, it meant help people. I've done my best to do that and have been rewarded with a great family, wonderful friends, and financial security.

The last voice message, when I was sixty-four, said "We can communicate with you in many ways." I had recently been shown four examples of how the spirit world could take over my voice and my thoughts and my actions. I knew then that I'd always been their puppet to accomplish the things they wanted me to do.

Over the years I received other messages I call 'knowledge messages,' such as the time I was driving into Halfway for the first time and the thought, not the voice, came into my head letting me know "You've found home." I wasn't looking for another home, this was not my idea, but it turned out to be true.

The house in Halfway is also an example where possibilities seemed to fall into place of their own accord: Ruth Huff, our hostess when we visited Halfway, had failing health and Kathy and I were getting desperate to find our own place in Halfway, but there were no houses for sale in town. The original houses we made offers on sold for less than offered, yet no one contacted us to see if we still wanted them and now there were none available. We ended up buying a very rough piece of undeveloped property, and today, after thirty years, it has become exactly what we wanted, a retreat for us and a place for family to gather. Everything ended up in exactly the right place. None of the original houses we looked at could have done that.

I was trained by my grandfather to box, but boxing is not fighting, yet, in the case of the speeding car, I knew what to do when I had to defend myself from the guy that was hell-bent on hitting me, and I knew just how hard to hit him without doing any real damage. I knew how to cool down the guy who wanted to fight me at the gas dock.

I had no training as a professional diver, yet never had a failure.

In each case, I was guided to do the right thing.

In my early career, people helped me and my partners on faith—the managers at Croft & Neville, Medco, Crown Zellerbach, and the log buyer at Publishers, the banker at US Bank, the guy at the steel shop; people who gave us jobs or contracts, people who lent us money or let us buy critical items to start or grow our businesses on credit, even though we had no money and no track record. It all fell together. It was all interlocked.

I think this was finally hammered into my brain so strongly when the spirit world came and gave me the four experiences where they took over my mind, my body, and my voice—I was a puppet for them. Most people who don't know me, who don't know that I always tell the truth, would say I was a nutcase, and I wouldn't resent them for thinking so. But these experiences happened; they did it to show they could control and use me and they did control and use me to help other people. If we can't do something to help other people, what is the purpose of our lives? I think that's why we are here.

Chapter 56: Conclusions

I SEE THE spiritual world as two entities. The one we think of as God, which is the high authority. The layer between man and God is a spiritual layer, perhaps made up of the spirits of man. These spirits communicate with us. I feel that I have been given the gift of hearing these messages. Early on I responded correctly to the first messages so I received more messages.

I have been asking them, the spiritual, if I am supposed to be writing this book, but I haven't gotten a clear answer. However, I have a comfortable feeling that with the way the world is changing, that perhaps others are doing the same thing—writing and talking about experiences like mine—and it's time for man to become more connected—or reconnected—with the spiritual side.

Man needs this spiritual connection. I believe early on that all people had a spiritual connection. Predators have thick skin and big teeth and can run fast. Man needed a way to defend himself. He made tools and fire, but early cave man was just a slow piece of meat with no defenses. For early man to exist and make progress, he needed a spiritual guide to help tell him when danger was near. I think we have grown away from that spiritual connection—that we've ignored it too long and we've lost it. It's time to get it back. As a species, we are going to destroy ourselves if we don't. When you look at mankind throughout history, his life is a disaster with wars and killing. I don't think this is the way it's supposed to be. Why it's that way, I don't know. I think the solution is to listen to the guidance the spiritual gives us and let them use us to help people, to help ourselves, live a good life.

I became very successful in life. However, I cannot take credit for all the good I did or the projects that should have failed and were successful. Only in retrospect did I realize I had not accomplished many of the things I had on my own—and for which I had taken credit. I came to realize that I was being used, like a puppet, to make these things happen.

I was lying in bed one night and thought of the early days. I could see that it had been laid out for me; the spiritual was there all the time. As a young child, when scuba was in its infancy and not many people knew about it, before television showed us things going on in other parts of the world, I'd been told I'd be a professional diver and I was.

I was told my girlfriend, Sandy, was pregnant and we were able to get married without her mother ever knowing why.

In the first two years of my adulthood all of the experiences I would need for my career were presented to me:

At 17 I lied about my age and went to work in the woods, where I learned all I needed to know about logging. I worked on a landing loading trucks, behind a D8 Cat setting chokers, and with fallers. I learned about log scale and logging terminology like formula C. At Klamath Lake I was in the right place at the right time and got the chance to salvage a few logs. These experiences, end to end, gave me the knowledge and skills I needed to get the first log salvage job with Medco, which led to a successful log salvage business, which led to more successes.

After high school I went to work building an irrigation tunnel where I learned important lessons about working with men, officials and explosives; lessons I used when building a business, working with people, or eliminating deadly threats from the river.

At nineteen I moved to southern California where the voice told me I would work with Croft & Neville. There I learned to build docks and ramps and drive piles and did my first professional dives. With that information I built three marinas, designed a new concrete dock system, and became financially secure designing a new foam flotation system.

At age twenty I moved back to Oregon where I went to work for a carpenter and built homes. At the end of that job I stood back and told myself, *I can do that. I can build from the ground up.* With that knowledge I built the apartments that gave me the equity to buy my first moorage. By expanding that first moorage, Sportcraft Landing, and fighting to keep it in existence, I was able to provide access to the river to many people. With income from the foam business I was able to build Scappoose and Channel Moorages. With the income from the moorages I was able to develop the property at Halfway and am able to live a comfortable life that will continue to provide income to my family when I am gone.

I believe none of this was by chance. The spiritual was guiding me and, perhaps, guiding others—like the managers at Croft & Neville, Medco and Crown Zellerbach—to give me opportunities without knowing me or my abilities.

I worked in some very dangerous and difficult situations. I could have died on my first dive when I was carrying too much weight on a jury-rigged tank that wasn't full. We could have lost my business partner Keith's brother in the pontoon fire. The ineptitude of the engineering manager at the paper mill on the California coast provided many opportunities to kill us. The salvage jobs I did for Devine's were full of danger. I believe the spiritual was there to make these efforts successful and keep anyone from getting seriously hurt.

When I broke my leg Kathy was there to be sure I received proper medical care and didn't lose my leg. She was in my life as the direct result of the voice telling me to raise her boys. In addition, I gained two more great sons.

When I asked how I could show my appreciation for all the help they had given me, the voice told me, "People." Many of my decisions, such as giving up building apartments in order to give people access to the river through Sportcraft, have been my way of showing my appreciation. In return, I've never worried where the money would come from; when I needed it, it was there. That isn't to say I didn't keep working hard all the time, I did and I still do.

Even with no money, I never went seriously hungry. I don't have any special skills handling a rifle, but I was consistently successful hunting deer and able to feed many people who may not otherwise have had meat to feed their families. Of all the members of our hunting parties, I was the one consistently guided to where deer were hidden in the brush and positioned exactly right to make a killing shot. Many of these shots were what I call "subliminal shots"—I had no conscious knowledge a deer was there or of taking aim at any particular part of the deer, but I was successful too many times to believe I found the deer or made the shots on my own. When I asked the spiritual how I could make these miracle shots they responded with, "What did you do with the meat?" I'd been used to feed others, to help people.

Everyone's spiritual experiences are different. Mine have all been positive.

Over time, there was a change in the type of messages—from a voice with words to a voice without words—a knowledge message instead of a spoken one.

I knew when I saw Halfway for the first time that I'd found home, even when I wasn't aware of looking for a home. I knew deer and coyotes were in a certain place at a certain time when I could not have known it from my own knowledge. I knew how to solve complex salvage problems without any specialized technical training, and how to do it without anyone being seriously injured.

I think the spiritual were there at other times, too, without saying anything.

I was there on Fred Devine's last dive and he was able to see the type of work I could do, which led to my working as a professional diver for Devine's.

On salvage jobs, like the one in Aleutian Islands or the one in the Arctic Ocean, we had to make do with the materials we could find. Even in these very remote areas what we needed was always there. It all worked. Always. Because of my belief in the spiritual connection, I believe they were there, quietly at work. They helped to save investors millions of dollars and kept anyone from being seriously hurt.

I was available, I was vulnerable, I was willing, and I could do what they wanted. I was given opportunities in a logical sequence and I acted on them. In return, I was amply rewarded. I think my life proves it. It's a good way to live a life.

Only once did I fail to respond to the voice in a timely manner, there was an accident and someone died. For a number of years the voice did not speak to me. I asked the spiritual if I was out of favor and they gave me the four examples showing me they didn't need to use a voice—they told me where a deer or coyote would be when I could not have known it on my own; they made me state this knowledge, with conviction, to others when I had no intention of saying anything. They told me, "We can communicate with you in many ways." Then I knew they could take over my voice and my mind and my body. Then I knew they had been there all the time.

As a young man, when I was finally able to see this, that a spiritual presence was guiding my life, I wondered if I could use this gift to see into the future. As I formed the thought, I received the vision of a tunnel with a blockage in it; a tunnel that represented my life and the knowledge that change was coming. That vision came true.

I was twenty-six years old before I told anyone about the voices and my belief in a spiritual presence that guides us. I was afraid no one would believe me, so I made a vow to never tell another lie. That way, people who knew me would know I was telling the truth. After a year of always telling the truth, I tested the waters. If I found someone I thought I could reveal my experiences with the spirit world to, I would tell them a little bit about my experiences. If it went well, I'd tell them more. I am amazed at how many people say, "Yeah, I've had an experience like that, too." Most of these people had one experience, not many as I have.

From listening to their stories, it seems to me that the ones who hear the voice a second time are the ones who responded to the first voice. I believe that if they, the spiritual, do not get a firm, positive reaction the first time they contact us, they move on to someone who is more receptive.

Except for one time, I immediately responded to all the messages I received. In that way, I was letting the spirit world know I was useful to them, that they could use me to get things done. When a person is receptive, like I was, the spiritual will use that person to help other people with whom they, the spiritual, do not have a strong link.

However, hearing the voice too much can be dangerous to humans. It is addictive. It should be used as a guide, not a way to run your life. My thinking is that a person could destroy their life waiting for a voice or message or sign to tell them what to do. Just think, if you could ask a question in your mind and have a spiritual voice answer it, you would stop functioning on your own. In order to function, you need to solve your own problems.

I was very successful in my careers and believe I was guided to these successes, but I had to do the work. The spiritual led me to know that money is not the important thing. Of course, you need to make enough to be comfortable, but too much money is not good for people. What is important is doing what you should be doing, or what you like doing, as opposed to what money dictates. What you do for others is more important than how much money you make. I could have stayed building apartments, but I would have been going against what I knew I should be doing. I've never regretted selling the apartments and putting the money into Sportcraft Landing and giving people access to the river they love. I enjoyed it. I didn't want to be wealthy. I did very well in my professional life and ended up with some assets and that's good, but the most important thing is people: Friends, family and the people you deal with. When I asked, "What can I do to show my appreciation for all I've been given?" The voice said, "People." Helping people is the key.

Anyone who knows me knows I always tell the truth, but I do not expect everyone to share my belief in a spiritual presence that communicates directly with us and, if they don't, that's fine. If someone doesn't know me and thinks what I have to say is bullshit, that I'm making it all up, I'm fine with that, too. However, I think there is enough proof in what I've experienced to make it clear that a spiritual presence does exist.

It opens up a new area of thought that, for whatever reason, there is something guiding me, guiding all of us. This is very useful to know. If you are struggling to do the right thing for the right reason, there is help. It doesn't always come in a voice and it may not be in an obvious way. There are many ways we receive messages. We receive help. We just have to learn to listen and to follow their guidance; we need to keep going in the right direction.

THE END

Postscript

(As we were wrapping up this book, Ken shared this story with me. I think it is a good example of how, even in little ways, he tries to make the world better for others.)

IN MARCH 2013 I had some memory tests to see where my brain is damaged. It's not debilitating like a stroke, but I was some memory issues. I was a few minutes early. Pretty soon this guy with a billed cap, who doesn't look anything like a doctor, came in.

"Are you Mr. Dye?" he asked me, a grouchy look on his face.

Great, I thought, *I'm in for four hours with this old fart.* I was in a pretty good mood and figured, *I'm going to change this.*

In one of the tests he said, "I'm going to read a paragraph out of a story. I want you to remember it and after a bit I'm going to ask you to repeat it."

I couldn't do it. As he was telling the story, it had no meaning. If he told me a hunting story, or something interesting, I think I would have remembered it. Who knows, I may have always been this way. I wasn't good at this stuff in school, either. I was good at looking at figures and putting them together. When we were tested in high school, I had to take figures (shapes) and build it in my mind. I did them all in the time allotted except the last one, but all the rest were right—the examiner said it was the highest score she'd ever seen.

Right away I found an opportunity to kid around with this grumpy old doctor. If I couldn't do something right, I made fun of myself. By the time it was all done, he was laughing.

"Have you ever had a customer come in here and try to cheer you up?" I asked.

"No," he admitted.

"For me to whine about these little memory problems after all I've been given would be a little disrespectful to the spiritual side," I said.

He agreed.

I did okay in the tests, but wasn't as quick in my mind as I used to be. I also had a sonogram of my heart. The doctor thinks perhaps my heart is throwing out little clots that end up in my brain. I've had two small clots between the back lobe of the brain, which is used for memories, and the front lobe, which utilizes this knowledge, and the blockages are affecting my memory. It feels good to be writing this book while I still can!